RISKING THE FUTURE

Adolescent Sexuality, Pregnancy, and Childbearing

STATISTICAL APPENDIXES

Sandra L. Hofferth and
Cheryl D. Hayes, Editors

Panel on Adolescent Pregnancy
and Childbearing

Committee on Child Development
Research and Public Policy

Commission on Behavioral and
Social Sciences and Education

National Research Council

NATIONAL ACADEMY PRESS
Washington, D.C. 1987

National Academy Press • **2101 Constitution Avenue, NW** • **Washington, DC 20418**

NOTICE: The project that is the subject of this publication was approved by the Governing Board of the National Research Council, whose members are drawn from the councils of the National Academy of Sciences, the National Academy of Engineering, and the Institute of Medicine.

The National Research Council was established by the National Academy of Sciences in 1916 to associate the broad community of science and technology with the Academy's purposes of furthering knowledge and of advising the federal government. The Council operates in accordance with general policies determined by the Academy under the authority of its congressional charter of 1863, which established the Academy as a private, nonprofit, self-governing membership corporation. The Council has become the principal operating agency of both the National Academy of Sciences and the National Academy of Engineering in the conduct of their services to the government, the public, and the scientific and engineering communities. It is administered jointly by both Academies and the Institute of Medicine. The National Academy of Engineering and the Institute of Medicine were established in 1964 and 1970, respectively, under the charter of the National Academy of Sciences.

This project was sponsored by the Ford Foundation, the Rockefeller Foundation, the William and Flora Hewlett Foundation, the Robert Wood Johnson Foundation, and the Charles Stewart Mott Foundation. The interpretations and conclusions contained in this publication represent the views of the panel and not necessarily those of the sponsoring foundations, their trustees, or officers.

Printed in the United States of America

Panel on Adolescent Pregnancy and Childbearing

DANIEL D. FEDERMAN (Chair), Harvard Medical School
WENDY H. BALDWIN, Center for Population Research, National Institute of Child Health and Human Development
EZRA C. DAVIDSON, JR., Department of Obstetrics and Gynecology, Charles R. Drew Postgraduate Medical School
JOY G. DRYFOOS, Hastings-on-Hudson, New York
JACQUELINE D. FORREST, Alan Guttmacher Institute, New York
FRANK F. FURSTENBERG, JR., Department of Sociology, University of Pennsylvania
BEATRIX A. HAMBURG, Mt. Sinai School of Medicine, City University of New York
RICHARD JESSOR, Institute of Behavioral Science, University of Colorado
JUDITH E. JONES, Center for Population and Family Health, Columbia University
FRANK LEVY, School of Public Affairs, University of Maryland
ROBERT H. MNOOKIN, Stanford Law School
KRISTIN A. MOORE, Child Trends, Inc., Washington, D.C.
ROSS D. PARKE, Department of Psychology, University of Illinois
HAROLD A. RICHMAN, Chapin Hall Center for Children, National Opinion Research Center, University of Chicago
MARIS VINOVSKIS, Department of History, University of Michigan

CHERYL D. HAYES, Study Director
SANDRA L. HOFFERTH, Adviser
MARGARET E. ENSMINGER, Consultant
DEE ANN L. WENK, Statistical Consultant
CELIA SHAPIRO, Staff Assistant

Committee on Child Development Research and Public Policy

WILLIAM A. MORRILL (Chair), Mathtech, Inc., Princeton
WILLIAM KESSEN (Vice Chair), Department of Psychology, Yale University
EUGENE S. BARDACH, School of Public Policy, University of California, Berkeley
DONALD T. CAMPBELL, Department of Social Relations, Lehigh University
DAVID L. CHAMBERS, School of Law, University of Michigan
FELTON EARLS, School of Medicine, Washington University, St. Louis
DORIS R. ENTWISLE, Department of Social Relations, Johns Hopkins University
FRANK F. FURSTENBERG, JR., Department of Sociology, University of Pennsylvania
HERBERT GINSBURG, Department of Human Development, Columbia University
SHEILA B. KAMERMAN, School of Social Work, Columbia University
LUIS M. LAOSA, Educational Testing Service, Princeton, N.J.
SAMUEL J. MESSICK, Educational Testing Service, Princeton, N.J.
JOHN MODELL, Department of History and Philosophy, Carnegie-Mellon University
T.M. JIM PARHAM, School of Social Work, University of Georgia
MICHAEL L. RUTTER, Institute of Psychiatry, University of London
EUGENE SMOLENSKY, Department of Economics, University of Wisconsin
BARBARA STARFIELD, School of Medicine, Johns Hopkins University
CAROL K. WHALEN, School of Social Ecology, University of California, Irvine
DANIEL D. FEDERMAN (ex officio), Chair, Panel on Adolescent Pregnancy and Childbearing

Contents

FOREWORD vii
PREFACE xi

Adolescent Pregnancy and Childbearing: An Emerging Research Focus *Cheryl D. Hayes* 1

Influences on Early Sexual and Fertility Behavior

1 Factors Affecting Initiation of Sexual Intercourse
   Sandra L. Hofferth 7

2 Adolescent Sexual Behavior As It Relates to Other Transition Behaviors in Youth *Margaret E. Ensminger* 36

3 Contraceptive Decision-Making Among Adolescents
   Sandra L. Hofferth 56

4 Teenage Pregnancy and Its Resolution *Sandra L. Hofferth* 78

Consequences of Early Sexual and Fertility Behavior

5 The Health and Medical Consequences of Adolescent Sexuality and Pregnancy: A Review of the Literature
   Donna M. Strobino 93

6 Social and Economic Consequences of Teenage Childbearing *Sandra L. Hofferth* 123

7 Teenage Fatherhood *Ross D. Parke and Brian Neville* 145

8 The Children of Teen Childbearers *Sandra L. Hofferth* 174

Programs and Policies

9 The Effects of Programs and Policies on Adolescent Pregnancy and Childbearing *Sandra L. Hofferth* 207

10 Estimates of Public Costs for Teenage Childbearing: A Review of Recent Studies and Estimates of 1985 Public Costs   *Martha R. Burt with Frank Levy* 264

REFERENCES 295

STATISTICAL APPENDIX   Trends in Adolescent Sexual and Fertility Behavior   *Kristin A. Moore, DeeAnn Wenk, Sandra L. Hofferth, and Cheryl D. Hayes, editors* A1/353

Foreword

Adolescent pregnancy and childbearing are matters of substantial national concern. Even the analysis and description of these phenomena, much less prescriptions for altering present trends, are highly controversial. And it is all too easy to avoid or to deal only obliquely with issues that arouse so many deep-seated emotions and convictions. There is, nonetheless, broad agreement that the personal and public costs resulting from unintended pregnancies and untimely birth are far too high to countenance an indifferent response. Discontinued educations, reduced employment opportunities, unstable marriages (if they occur at all), low incomes, and heightened health and developmental risks to the children of adolescent mothers are a few of the most obvious and immediate personal costs. Sustained poverty, frustration, and hopelessness are all too often the long-term outcomes. Furthermore, the welfare, Medicaid, and Food Stamp program costs in 1985 for families begun by a birth to a teenager reached $16.65 billion.

Programs and services to prevent pregnancy and improve the life chances of teenage parents and their children have appeared in increasing number since the mid-1970s, frequently stirring up powerful or vocal advocates and opponents. An ever more impassioned debate has drawn public, private, voluntary, and philanthropic organizations into a continuing pursuit for "solutions" to the perceived problems. Yet, after more than a decade of experience, there seemed to many observers an imbalance in emphasis between what people believed and what policy makers, professionals, and society in general knew about the impacts and cost-effectiveness of alternative prevention and amelioration strategies in light of better scientific knowledge about early sexual and fertility behavior. There seemed to be distressingly little discussion about how various interventions work, for whom, under what circumstances, and with what intended and unintended effects. And what were the most promising directions for future policy and program development?

In 1983, at the urging of several of its members, the Committee on Child Development Research and Public Policy within the National Research Council proposed the establishment of a study panel to conduct a broad and dispassionate review of relevant research and program experience and to recommend approaches for policy formulation, program design, research, and evaluation. In 1984, with generous support from five foundations—the Rockefeller Foundation, the Ford Foundation, the William and Flora Hewlett Foundation, the Robert Wood Johnson Foundation, and the Charles Stewart Mott Foundation—the Panel on Adolescent Pregnancy and Childbearing began its study. Over a two-year period, this broadly interdisciplinary 15-person panel and its staff and consultants undertook three major tasks: (1) to assemble, integrate, and assess data on trends in teenage sexual and fertility behavior; (2) to review and synthesize research on the antecedents and consequences of early pregnancy and childbearing; and (3) to review alternative preventive and ameliorative policies and programs.

In meeting its charge, the panel developed two volumes. Volume I presents the panel's findings, conclusions, and recommendations. Detailed background reviews of existing research on factors affecting the initiation of sexual intercourse, contraceptive use, pregnancy and pregnancy resolution, and the consequences of teenage pregnancy, childbearing, and parenting for young mothers, fathers, and their children, as well as the costs and effects of policies and programs, constitute Volume II. Also included in Volume II is a comprehensive statistical appendix presenting data from a variety of sources on trends in teenage sexual and fertility behavior. Throughout Volume I the panel refers to the papers and the statistical appendix in Volume II to support its deliberations. The panel based its study on both existing information and new analyses of existing data. These sources were supplemented by workshops and individual discussions with many federal, state, and local policy makers, program designers, service providers, and evaluators, as well as site visits to a variety of programs across the nation. In accordance with institutional policy, this report has been extensively and thoroughly reviewed by individuals other than members of the study panel.

In recent years, many other individuals and groups representing an array of moral, philosophical, and political perspectives have addressed the complex and controversial issues surrounding adolescent pregnancy. Many have developed recommendations and guidelines for policy makers, service providers, parents, and adolescents themselves. This report is one step in a continuing process of inquiry, review, and synthesis. As a scientific body, the Panel on Adolescent Pregnancy and Childbearing sought to clarify the issues, sharpen awareness of crucial decision points, and define the limits of existing knowledge. Although science cannot resolve issues that are inextricably bound to differences in human values, it can illuminate the trade-offs among different political and ideological positions, and we believe this report will inform the continuing public debate.

On behalf of the members of the parent Committee on Child Development Research and Public Policy, I would like to acknowledge the special contribution of Daniel D. Federman, who served as panel chair. His commitment of time, energy, and intellectual resources over the past two years has been extraordinary. In large part, the success of this study is due to his exquisite leadership. Acknowledgment is also due to the other members of the Panel on Adolescent Pregnancy and Childbearing. All gave generously of their time and knowledge throughout the study. As a diverse group of individuals, they are to be commended for producing a unanimous report on a topic that inevitably raises public controversy and stirs personal convictions.

The members of the panel join the committee in extending our great appreciation to the staff of the study. Cheryl D. Hayes, the study director for the panel as well as the parent committee, once again demonstrated the enormous energy, outstanding thoroughness, and great skill for which she is well known to many of us. Special thanks go also to Celia Shapiro, staff assistant to the committee and the panel, for her tireless attention to administrative detail throughout the study and for her patience and persistence in assembling the references for the two volumes. We gratefully acknowledge the significant contribution of Sandra L. Hofferth of the National Institute of Child Health and Human Development, who authored many of the research reviews that informed the panel's deliberations and coedited Volume II of the report. The efforts of Dee Ann Wenk of the University of Kentucky, who served as statistical consultant and worked with members of the panel and the staff in compiling the data and preparing the numerous tables and figures that appear in the report and the statistical appendix, are also gratefully acknowledged. Margaret A. Ensminger and Donna M. Strobino, both of Johns Hopkins University, served as consultants and authored thoughtful background papers that are included in Volume II. Finally, Christine L. McShane, editor for the Commission on Behavioral and Social Sciences and Education, edited the report with a critical eye and managed the final production of the volumes.

The panel has also benefited from the contributions of several individuals who prepared special tabulations of existing data to help it address a number of difficult issues that remain unresolved in the available research. Special thanks are due Frank Mott of the Center for Human Resource Research at Ohio State University, William Pratt, Marjorie Horn, Christine Bachrach, and Stephanie Ventura of the National Center for Health Statistics, and Stanley Henshaw of the Alan Guttmacher Institute. Many other individuals played an important role in the panel's deliberations by providing information, critical analysis, advice, and reviews of the draft report and the draft background papers. Their thoughtful comments and insights are reflected in the final manuscripts.

Finally, this study would not have been possible without the generous support of our foundation sponsors. On behalf of the Committee on Child Development Research and Public Policy, I would like to extend special thanks to Mary Kritz of the Rockefeller Foundation, Prudence Brown of the Ford Foundation, Anne Firth Murray of the William and Flora Hewlett Foundation, Paul Jellinek of the Robert Wood Johnson Foundation, and Marilyn Steele of the Charles Stewart Mott Foundation. Their encouragement and advice greatly enhanced the study at every stage.

WILLIAM A. MORRILL, Chair
Committee on Child Development
Research and Public Policy

Preface

No human experience is at once so transiently private and lastingly public as an unintended pregnancy. When the mother herself is a young adolescent, only partially educated and almost wholly economically dependent, the pregnancy is inevitably enmeshed in a ragged tapestry of personal, interpersonal, social, religious, ethical, and economic dimensions. The peculiarly human gap between reproductive maturation and social self-sufficiency sets the stage for the problem. Many factors beyond the control—even the ken—of the young people involved complicate the scene. At every point, external expectations batter on newly emerging drives, challenging young adolescents to balance immediate satisfaction and long-range consequences radically disproportionate from anything they have previously had to deal with. It is little wonder that in this very complicated arena research has been difficult and social consensus elusive.

Our panel was convened to collect, review, and evaluate the data on trends in adolescent pregnancy and childbearing and on the antecedents and consequences of this phenomenon and to initiate proposals for the evolution of potentially helpful programs. We had the generous support of five foundations: the Ford Foundation, the Rockefeller Foundation, the William and Flora Hewlett Foundation, the Robert Wood Johnson Foundation, and the Charles Stewart Mott Foundation, all of which have demonstrated a long-standing interest in issues associated with adolescent pregnancy and childbearing. Many have made substantial investments in a growing body of relevant research and a lengthening list of targeted programs. Their interest in this study—and indeed, as a panel of scholars and experts, our interest in undertaking it—is a concern about the problems of early unintended pregnancy and parenting in our society and what is known about how to effectively address them. Our sponsors were models of what scholars hope for—generous, supportive, and never intrusive. The project officers were consistently helpful, but at no time was any of our work constrained by the foundations nor beholden to them. The staff of the National Research Council was consistently supportive, and our study director, Cheryl Hayes, who also serves as executive officer of the parent Committee on Child Development Research and Public Policy, was at once a colleague, a paragon, and the principal drafter of the report.

Few people can approach the problem of teenage pregnancy dispassionately. Becoming sexually active, using contraception, considering abortion or adoption—every step is invested with a panoply of moral and religious questions, and these decisions are often undertaken alone by a frightened and immature young woman who would be considered a child in nearly any other context. A consciousness of this poignance pervades our report, and deliberately so. The panel believes that at each step—however much one may wish for a different outcome of a prior decision—the potentially or actually pregnant teenager should be treated kindly and warmly and should have a complete set of options available without the interposition of moral hounding or economic barriers.

In general, we believe preventive strategies should be given more public and private support than is now available. An international comparison study by the Alan Guttmacher Institute, of which the panel was beneficiary, provided valuable insight into the role of preventive services in countries of comparable levels of teenage sexual activity.

Many social circumstances are closely related to the problem of teenage pregnancy and childbearing. Youth unemployment, poverty, poor education, single-parent families, television content—all these and more are accompaniments and very likely determinants of the high rates of adolescent pregnancy in the United States. The hope for a solution to the problem of teenage pregnancy is illusory without simultaneous amelioration of some of these contributing factors. Pending such comprehensive change, the panel urges prevention rather than denial, kindness rather than exhortation, and research rather than doctrine.

DANIEL D. FEDERMAN, Chair
Panel on Adolescent
Pregnancy and Childbearing

STATISTICAL APPENDIX
TRENDS IN ADOLESCENT SEXUAL AND FERTILITY BEHAVIOR

Kristin A. Moore, DeeAnn Wenk, Sandra L. Hofferth,
and Cheryl D. Hayes, editors

The major purpose of this statistical appendix is to provide an integrated and comprehensive source of data on teenage fertility behavior. To date, much of the public data on prevalence of sexual activity by age, sex, race and cohort in the United States, as well as trends in pregnancies, births, abortions, marriage and adoption, have not been available in any single source. Much of the information presented in this statistical appendix was derived from data published by various federal government agencies, including the U.S. Bureau of Census and the National Center for Health Statistics. Much of it is also available in published form from non-governmental surveys. Some of the information presented here was derived from unpublished data made available by both governmental and non-governmental sources.

This statistical appendix is one part of a comprehensive examination of adolescent pregnancy and childbearing conducted by the Panel on Adolescent Pregnancy and Childbearing, under the auspices of the National Research Council's Committee on Child Development Research and Public Policy. The study was supported by a consortium of private foundations, including the Rockefeller Foundation, the Ford Foundation, the Robert Wood Johnson Foundation, the William and Flora Hewlett Foundation, and the Charles Stewart Mott Foundation. Over the two years of the study, the panel conducted a detailed review of data on trends in teenage sexual and fertility behavior, a review and synthesis of research on the antecedents and consequences of adolescent pregnancy and childbearing, and a review of intervention strategies and programs. The statistical appendix was prepared as background for the panel's report and as a reference for policy-makers, researchers, and others seeking information on patterns of sexual and fertility behavior among U.S. teenagers.

This appendix is organized according to the panel's conceptual scheme for understanding adolescent sexual decision making. The process of becoming an adolescent parent, beginning with the initiation of sexual intercourse, involves a series of decision points faced by all adolescents (see Volume I, Chapter 1). Choices (which vary in their degree of conscious decisionmaking) at each successive point in the sequence are dependent on the outcomes of previous choices. The total number and proportion of adolescents reaching each point in the decision-making process are determined by a variety of social and demographic factors.

The proportion of teenagers who are sexually active and the consistency of contraceptive use are the key factors that affect the probability of pregnancy in the adolescent population. Once a pregnancy occurs, the proportion of teenagers who voluntarily terminate their pregnancy, give birth in- or out-of-wedlock, or relinquish their child for adoption affects the number of teenagers who become parents and the number who become unmarried parents. A change in the size of the adolescent population or in any of these factors will ultimately produce a change in the number of adolescent parents. Thus, it is important to examine recent trends and current levels in the frequencies of an entire range of behaviors in order to understand trends in adolescent pregnancy and childbearing.

Additionally, adolescents are not a monolithic group. Adolescent behavior varies by age, sex, race, ethnicity and socioeconomic characteristics. For this reason, we have endeavored to provide data by age categories (i.e., less than 15 years old, 15 to 17 years old, and 18 to 19 years old) by race and ethnicity, and by sex. In some cases, however, data were not available in the desired form. Often, for example, age categories were inconsistent over time and across sources. Some data were not available by race and ethnicity. Despite these difficulties, we have tried to provide as much information as possible while retaining the ability to make meaningful comparisons of data from different sources and over time. In many cases data for older age groups are presented for comparison with adolescent age groups.

The statistical appendix is organized into eight sections containing tables with brief accompanying summaries. Sections 1 through 4 present data on teenagers at successive points along the path to adolescent pregnancy, including sexual activity, contraceptive use, and premarital pregnancy. Sections 5 through 7 present data on teenagers choosing different resolutions to pregnancy including abortion, marriage, birth, and adoption. The final section contains information on adolescents who became parents.

This appendix is not intended to be analytical. The earlier chapters of Volume II provide a more complete synthesis of the research literature, an assessment of the reliability of the data, and an identification of gaps in available knowledge. The addendum to this volume contains detailed descriptions of the major sources of data used for constructing the tables.

TABLES

I. <u>SEXUAL ACTIVITY AMONG ADOLESCENTS</u>

1.1   Proportion Of Women Aged 15 To 19 Beginning Menstruation At Specific Ages, By Race, 1976 - 1980

1.2   Percent Never Married Women Living In Metropolitan Areas Ever Experiencing Sexual Intercourse, By Age 1971 - 1982

1.3   All Women And Never-Married Women Who Have Ever Had Sexual Intercourse, By Age And Race, 1982, National Survey Of Family Growth

1.4   Cumulative Sexual Activity By Single Year Of Age, Sex, Race And Ethnicity, 1983, National Longitudinal Survey Of Youth

1.5   Cumulative Percentage Of Women And Men Under 20 Who Ever Had Intercourse, By Age, Race And Study, United States, 1938 to 1984

1.6   Percent of Sexually Experienced Never-Married Women Aged 15-19 Who Had Intercourse Only Once, by Age and Race, 1976

1.7   Frequency Of Sexual Intercourse Among Unmarried Females 15 To 24 Who Ever Had Intercourse By Race, 1982 National Survey Of Family Growth

1.8   Distribution (in Percentages) Of Total Number Of Premarital Sexual Partners, By Race: 1971, 1976 And 1979 - Sexually Experienced Females Aged 15 to 19, Metropolitan U.S.

1.9   Percentage Distribution Of Women Aged 15-19 And Of Men Aged 17-21, By Relationship With Their First Sexual Partner, According To Race, 1979, Metropolitan U.S.

1.10 Percentage Distribution Of Women Aged 15-19 And Of Men Aged 17-21, By Relationship With Their First Sexual Partner, According To Age At First Intercourse, 1979, Metropolitan U.S.

1.11   Percentage Distribution Of Locale Of First Premarital Intercourse, Women Aged 15-19, By Race, 1976 And 1979, Metropolitan U.S.

1.12   Estimated Cummulative Percent Ever Experiencing Sexual Intercourse By Single Year of Age, Race, Ethnicity And Mother's Education, 1983, National Longitudinal Survey of Youth

1.13   Cumulative Sexual Activity By Single Year Of Age And By Drop Out Rate Of Respondent's High School, 1979 From National Longitudinal Survey Of Youth

II. CONTRACEPTIVE USE AMONG ADOLESCENTS

2.1   Percentage Distribution Of Sexually Active Women Aged 15-19, By Contraceptive-Use Status, According To Race, 1976, 1979, 1982

2.2   Percent Of Women Aged 15-44 Who Used A Contraceptive Method At First Intercourse And Percent Distribution Of Women Who Used A Method, By Type Of Method, 1982 National Survey Of Family Growth

2.3   Percentage Distribution Of Sexually Experienced Women Aged 15-19 And Men Aged 17-21, By Type Of Contraceptive Method Used At First Intercourse; Percentage Distribution Of Those Using A Method, By Type Of Method; According To Race And Planning Status Of First Intercourse, 1979, Metropolitan U.S.

2.4   Percentage Distribution Of Sexually Experienced Women Aged 15-19 By Type of Contraceptive Method Used At First Intercourse; Percentage Distribution Of Those Using A Method, By Type Of Method; According To Race, 1982 National Survey Of Family Growth

2.5   Percentage Distribution Of Sexually Experienced Women Aged 15-19 And Men Aged 17-21 Who Did Not Use A Contraceptive Method At First Intercourse, By Reason Reported For Not Having Used A Method, According To Planning Status Of First Intercourse And Race, 1979, Metropolitan U.S.

2.6   Percent Of Sexually Active Unmarried Women Under Age 20 By Timing Of First Contraception And Age At First Intercourse, According To Race, 1982, National Survey Of Family Growth

2.7   Number of Women Aged 15-44 Exposed To The Risk Of Unintended Pregnancy, And Percentage Currently Practicing Contraception, By Marital Status, by Age, National Survey Of Family Growth

2.8 Number Of Never Married Women 15-44 Years Of Age Who Were Exposed To The Risk Of An Unintended Pregnancy, And Percent Using A Method Of Contraception, By Race And Age, And Percent Distribution Of Contraceptors By Method Of Contraception, According To Race And Age: United States, 1982

2.9 Number And Percentage Distribution Of Hispanic And Non-Hispanic Women Aged 15 To 19 (All Marital Statuses) Currently Exposed To The Risk Of Unintended Pregnancy By Current Contraceptive Status, 1982 National Survey of Family Growth

2.10 Percent Of Never-Married Women Aged 15-19 Who Correctly Perceived The Time Of Greatest Pregnancy Risk Within The Menstrual Cycle, By Age, Race And Sexual Experience, 1976 And 1971

2.11 Standardized Contraceptive-Use Failure Rates By User Characteristics And Method Type: Single Women, January 1, 1979-July 1, 1982

III. PREGNANCY AMONG ADOLESCENTS

3.1 Reproductive Behavior, U.S. Women Aged 15-19, 1960-1984

3.2 Pregnancies, Abortions, Miscarriages And Live Births By Marital Status To Women Aged 15 To 19, 1982

3.3 Proportion Of Women Ever-Pregnant Before Age 20, 1976 And 1981

3.4 Percentage of Premaritally Sexually Active Women Aged 15-19 Who Ever Experienced A Premarital First Pregnancy, By Contraceptive-Use Status And Race, 1979 And 1976, Metropolitan U.S.

3.5 Estimated Cumulative Percent Of Metropolitan-Area Females Aged 15-19 With Premarital First Pregnancy, By Duration Since First Intercourse, Race And Contraceptive Use Status, U.S., 1979

3.6 Percentage Distributions Of Women Aged 15-19 Who Ever Experienced A Premarital First Pregnancy And Were Unmarried At The Time The Pregnancy Was Resolved, By Pregnancy Intention And, Among Those Who Did Not Want The Pregnancy, By Contraceptive Use, According To Race, 1979, 1976 And 1971 (Metropolitan-Area Teenagers)

IV. INDUCED ABORTION AMONG ADOLESCENTS

4.1 Number And Percentage Distribution Of Legal Abortions, Abortion Rate Per 1,000 Women, And Percentage Of Pregnancies Terminated By Abortion, By Age Of Women, United States, Selected Years, 1974-1982

4.2 Percent Change In Abortion Rates And In The Number Of Pregnancies Terminated By Abortions By Age Group, 1974 To 1978, 1979 To 1981, 1981 To 1982

4.3 Abortion Rate Per 1,000 Women, By Age-group And Race, According To Marital Status, 1979-1981

4.4 Estimated Abortion Rate Per 1,000 Women Aged 12-19 By Race, United States, 1971-1978

4.5 Legal Abortions Per 1,000 Births (Abortion Ratio) By Age At Conception And By Race, United States, 1972-1978

4.6 Ratios of Induced Terminations of Pregnancy By Race And Age Of Woman, 1980: 12-State Area

4.7 Percent of Induced Terminations of Pregnancy To Women With No Previous Induced Termination, By Age And Race Of Women: 12-State Area, 1980

V. MARRIAGE AMONG PREGNANT ADOLESCENTS

5.1 Percent Of Males And Females Aged 15 to 19 Never-married, By Race And Ethnicity, 1960-1985

5.2 Percentage Of First-Born Babies Born to Mothers Aged 15-19 Conceived Either Maritally or Extra-Maritally, By Race, Age, and Marital Status at First Birth According To Birth Cohort Of Baby

VI. CHARACTERISTICS OF BIRTHS TO ADOLESCENTS

6.1 Number Of Births In The United States To Women Under Age 20 By Race, 1955 - 1984

6.2 Birth Rates By Age Of Mother, By Race Of Child, United States, 1950 - 1984

6.3 Number Of Out-Of-Wedlock Births In The United States (estimated) By Age Of Mother: 1955-1984

6.4 Birth Rates For Unmarried Women by Age of Mother and Race of Child: United States, 1970-84

6.5 Live Births By Age Of Father, Age Of Mother, And Race Of Child: United States, 1983

6.6 Percent Of All First Births And Total Births In Which The Mother's Age Was Under 20, Under 18 Or Under 15, By Race, United States, 1950-1984

6.7 Number and Percent of All Live Births to Women Under Age 20 by Hispanic Origin of Mother: Total of 23 Reporting States and the District of Columbia, 1984

6.8 Number and Percent of All Out of Wedlock Births to Women Under Age 20 by Hispanic Origin of Mother: Total of 23 Reporting States and the District of Columbia, 1984

6.9 Percentage Of Mothers Receiving Inadequate Prenatal Care, By Age Group According To Race And Ethnicity, Residence And Marital Status, National Natality Survey 1980

6.10 Number and Percent Of Live Births With Low Birth Weight and Live Births by Birth Weight, by Age of Mother and Race of Child: United States, 1983; Based On 100 Percent Of Births In Selected States And On A 50-Percent Sample Of Births In All Other States

6.11 Estimated Cumulative Percent of Women Aged 15 to 19 Ever Experiencing First Birth By Single Year of Age, Race, and Ethnicity, 1982 National Survey of Family Growth

6.12 Cumulative Percent Having A First Birth By Single Year Of Age, Race And Ethnicity, And By Mother's Education, Education in 1979; 1983 National Longitudinal Survey of Youth

6.13 Infant Mortality Rates (deaths at less than one year of age per 1,000 live births) By Age of Mother, U.S. Study of Infant Mortality from Linked Records and 1980 National Natality Survey/National Death Index (NNS/NDI)

VII. <u>ADOPTION OF CHILDREN BORN TO ADOLESCENTS</u>

7.1 Percentage Distribution Of Premarital Live Births Resulting From First Pregnancies Of Women Aged 15-19 At Interview, By Living Arrangements Of Baby And Race Of Mother: 1982, 1976, and 1971

7.2 Percentage Of Babies Born Premaritally To Women 15-44 Years Of Age At Interview Who Were Placed For Adoption By Age Of Mother At Birth Of Child And Race, 1982 National Survey of Family Growth

7.3 Adoptions by Type and Age of Mother, State of California Selected Years, 1967 to 1983

VIII. CHARACTERISTICS OF ADOLESCENT PARENTS

8.1 Percent of Women Aged 20-29 Completing High School By Age At Birth Of First Child, Race And Ethnicity, 1982 National Survey of Family Growth

8.2 Percent of Mothers Aged 20-29 Having A Subsequent Birth Within 24 Months Of The First, By Their Age at First Birth, Race And Ethnicity, 1982 National Survey of Family Growth

8.3 Cumulative Percentage Of Metropolitan-area Women Aged 15-19 Who Had A Premarital Second Pregnancy, By Number Of Months Following Outcome Of The Premarital First Pregnancy, According To Race, Outcome And Age At Conclusion Of First Pregnancy, 1971, 1976 and 1979

8.4 Receipt Of AFDC Among Women Aged 20-29 By The Women's Age At First Birth, Race, And Ethnicity, 1982 National Survey Of Family Growth

8.5 Poverty Status Of Mothers Aged 20-29, By Their Age At First Birth, Race, and Ethnicity, 1982 National Survey of Family Growth

I. SEXUAL ACTIVITY AMONG ADOLESCENTS

This section presents information on sexual activity among adolescents in the United States. Data are provided on sexual activity among never-married teens and married teens before and after marriage. In most cases the designation of being sexually active pertains to men and women ever having intercourse. Data are also provided on frequency of sexual intercourse, number of premarital sexual partners, location of first intercourse and other factors that may affect the timing of first sexual intercourse among adolescents, such as age at first menstruation.

The data came from three main sources, the National Surveys of Young Women and Men (NSYW/M), the National Longitudinal Surveys of Youth (NLS), and the National Survey of Family Growth (NSFG). The 1979 NSYW/M are for U.S. metropolitan areas only. For this reason the data in Table 1.2 from the 1971 and the 1976 NSYW/M and the 1982 NSFG were adjusted to include metropolitan areas only, in order to present a comparable time series. In subsequent tables for which similar data from the 1982 NSFG were not available, only data from the NSYW/M are presented. Data on young men are only available in the NSYM and the NLS.

The estimates of female sexual activity based on data from the NLS and the NSFG although generally consistent, differ in three respects. First, the age categories for the NSFG are mid-year (i.e., age 15 means 15.5 years) whereas for the NLS data, the age categories extend to the end of a specified age (i.e., age 15 means until the 16th birthday). Second, unless otherwise noted data from the NLS include all women regardless of marital status. Third, Hispanic persons in the NLS data may be of any race (black or white); in the NSFG data, unless otherwise noted black and white totals include Hispanic persons. This means that the race and ethnicity categories are not mutually exclusive. The NSYW/M do not include data on Hispanics.

TABLE 1.1 Proportion Of Women Aged 15 To 19 Beginning Menstruation At Specific Ages, By Race Of Women, 1976 - 1980[1]

Age at First Menstrual Cycle	Proportion of Women, by Race		
	Total	Whites	Blacks
8-10	5.1%	4.6%	7.6%
11	12.7	12.1	17.6
12	29.4	29.6	24.7
13	30.2	31.4	25.8
14	13.1	12.9	14.8
15	5.9	5.8	
16	2.9	2.9	9.5
17+	0.7	0.7	
	100.0	100.0	100.0
Mean Age	12.6	12.7	12.5
N =	2,121	1,767	305

Notes: None of the black-white differences in age at menarche reach accepted levels of statistical significance. The total group includes 49 women of other race groups. Where cell sizes fell below 25, data are grouped in categories.

[1]Data are derived from women's responses to a question in the medical interview, "How old were you when your period or menstrual cycles started? Data were coded in years.

Source: Unpublished tabulation from Ronette Briefel, National Center for Health Statistics, DHHS, Second National Health and Nutrition Examination Survey, 1976 - 1980.

TABLE 1.1

Table 1.1 shows the proportion of women aged 15 to 19 (studied between 1976 and 1980) by age at menarche and race. These data were tabulated from the Second National Health and Nutrition Survey. Over three quarters, 77.4 percent, of all women began menstruation by age 13, 96.4 percent of all women began menstruation by age 15. The mean age at first menstruation for all women was 12.6 years, 12.7 years for white women and 12.5 years for black women. The difference in age at first menstruation between black and white women is not statistically significant.

TABLE 1.2 Percent Never Married Women Living In Metropolitan Areas Ever Experiencing Sexual Intercourse, By Age 1971 - 1982 (percent who have had intercourse)

Race and Age	1982	1979	1976	1971	Percent Change 1971-82
All Races*					
15-19	42.2	46.0	39.2	27.6	52.9
15	17.8	22.5	18.6	14.4	23.6
16	28.1	37.8	28.9	20.9	34.4
17	41.0	48.5	42.9	26.1	57.0
18	52.7	56.9	51.4	39.7	32.7
19	61.7	69.0	59.5	46.4	33.0
White					
15-19	40.3	42.3	33.6	23.2	73.7
15	17.3	18.3	13.8	11.3	53.1
16	26.9	35.4	23.7	17.0	58.0
17	39.5	44.1	36.1	20.2	95.5
18	48.6	52.6	46.0	35.6	36.5
19	59.3	64.9	53.6	40.7	45.7
Black					
15-19	52.9	64.8	64.3	52.4	1.0
15	23.2	41.1	38.9	31.2	-25.6
16	36.3	50.4	55.1	44.4	-18.2
17	46.7	73.3	71.0	58.9	-20.7
18	75.7	76.3	76.2	60.2	25.7
19	78.0	88.5	83.9	78.3	- .4

*Includes races other than Black and White.

Sources: Melvin Zelnik & John F. Kantner, "Sexual Activity, Contraceptive Use amd Pregnancy Among Metropolitan-Area Teenagers: 1971-1979", <u>Family Planning Perspectives</u>, Vol. 12, No. 5, Sept/Oct 1980. William Pratt, NCHS, National Survey of Family Growth, 1982, Cycle III, unpublished tabulations, 1984.

TABLE 1.2

Table 1.2 shows the percent of never married women aged 15 to 19 living in metropolitan areas who had ever experienced sexual intercourse by 1971, 1976, 1979 and 1982. For all 15- to 19-year-old metropolitan women, there was a 53 percent increase in the percent of sexually experienced females between 1971 and 1982 due primarily to increases among whites. Overall, the percent increase in the proportion sexually experienced was the largest among 17-year olds. There was also a substantial increase in the proportion of females aged 15 and 16 who were sexually experienced.

Although the proportion sexually active increased during the 1970s, between 1979 and 1982, there was a slight decrease in the percent of metropolitan teenage females experiencing intercourse. Of women aged 15 to 19 in 1982, about 42 percent had had intercourse compared to 46 percent of women aged 15 to 19 in 1979. The decline in the proportion sexually active occurred for 15-, 16-, 17-, 18- and 19-year-old female teenagers regardless of race. The decline for white teenagers was slight, from 42.3 to 40.3 percent for 15- to 19-year-olds and is not statistically significant. The decline for black teenagers was much larger, from 64.8 to 52.9 percent for 15- to 19-year-olds. From a statistical perspective this trend is only marginally certain, and will have to be monitored to determine its significance.

It is important to note that, while more than 50 percent of females aged 18 to 19 in 1982 had experienced intercourse, fewer than 30 percent of females aged 15 and 16 in 1982 had done so.

TABLE 1.3 All Women And Never-Married Women Who Have Ever Had Sexual Intercourse, By Age And Race, 1982, National Survey Of Family Growth

Age*	Number of Women (1000s)			% Who Had Intercourse		
	Total**	White	Black	Total**	White	Black
All Women						
All Ages 15-44	54,099	45,367	6,985	86.3	86.0	89.7
15-19	9,521	7,815	1,416	46.9	44.9	58.9
15-17	5,122	4,119	821	32.2	30.1	44.1
15	1,474	1,191	209	19.2	17.9	28.0
16	1,601	1,302	260	30.4	28.8	41.6
17	2,046	1,626	352	43.0	40.1	55.4
18	2,327	1,967	302	58.1	54.8	77.0
19	2,072	1,728	293	70.7	69.0	82.0
20-24	10,629	8,855	1,472	85.4	84.5	93.2
25-44	33,949	28,697	4,097	97.6	97.7	99.0
Never-Married Women						
All Ages 15-44	19,164	14,948	3,545	61.3	57.6	79.6
15-19	8,839	7,193	1,377	42.8	40.2	57.8
15-17	4,968	3,971	818	30.1	27.5	43.8
15	1,460	1,177	209	18.4	16.9	28.0
16	1,559	1,263	257	28.5	26.7	40.8
17	1,949	1,531	352	40.1	36.4	55.4
18	2,107	1,768	289	53.8	49.7	76.1
19	1,764	1,454	270	65.6	63.2	80.5
20-24	5,811	4,502	1,084	73.3	69.5	90.8
25-44	4,514	3,252	1,084	82.0	79.7	96.3

*Single years of age refer to the mid-points in the age intervals, e.g., 15 means 15.5 years.

**Includes races other than White and Black.

Source: Pratt et al. "Understanding U.S. Fertility," Population Bulletin, Volume 39 No. 5, December 1984. Reprinted by permission.

TABLE 1.3

Table 1.3 shows data from the National Survey of Family Growth (NSFG) on the number and percent of all women and never married women who ever had sexual intercourse by age and race for 1982. Among all women aged 15 to 19, 47 percent had had sexual intercourse (44.9 percent of white teens and 58.9 percent of black teens), compared to more than 85 percent of all women older than age 20. The proportions of never-married women aged 15-19 ever having had sexual intercourse are only slightly lower than for all women aged 15 to 19 because most women under age 20 have never been married. Unmarried teens account for 32 percent of all unmarried women ever having had intercourse and 8 percent of all sexually active women.

It should be noted that the proportions presented in this table for never-married women differ slightly for those presented in Table 1.2 for 1982 because they are not limited to metropolitan areas.

TABLE 1.4 Cumulative Sexual Activity By Single Year Of Age, Sex, Race And Ethnicity1, 1983, National Longitudinal Survey Of Youth

	Cumulative % Sexually Active	
Age*	Male	Female
Total		
15	16.6	5.4
16	28.7	12.6
17	47.9	27.1
18	64.0	44.0
19	77.6	62.9
20	83.0	73.6
N	(4657)	(4648)
White		
15	12.1	4.7
16	23.3	11.3
17	42.8	25.2
18	60.1	41.6
19	75.0	60.8
20	81.1	72.0
N	(2828)	(2788)
Black		
15	42.4	9.7
16	59.6	20.1
17	77.3	39.5
18	85.6	59.4
19	92.2	77.0
20	93.9	84.7
N	(1146)	(1157)
Hispanics		
15	19.3	4.3
16	32.0	11.2
17	49.7	23.7
18	67.1	40.2
19	78.5	58.6
20	84.2	69.5
N	(683)	(703)

Note: Sample is limited to respondents age 20 and over at 1983 survey date.

*Percentages reference birthday for specified ages, e.g., 15 means by 15th birthday or end of 14.

1Hispanic persons may be of any race.

Source: Special Tabulations from the 1983 National Longitudinal Survey of Youth Center for Human Resource Research, Ohio State University.

TABLE 1.4

Data on the cumulative percent of males and females in the National Longitudinal Survey of Youth (NLS) who reported having had sexual intercourse are presented in Table 1.4. by age and race.

In all, 4 out of every 5 males and 7 out of every 10 females were sexually active by age 20. Among males, blacks were more likely to be sexually experienced than both Hispanic and white males. Nearly 60 percent of the black males had had intercourse by age 16 and 94 percent had had intercourse by age 20. In comparison, by age 16 about 32 percent of the Hispanic males and less than a quarter of the white males were sexually experienced. By age 20, slightly more than 80 percent of white and Hispanic males had had intercourse.

This data base, like the National Survey of Family Growth (NSFG), indicates that black females were more likely to have had intercourse than whites or Hispanics. Approximately 2 out of 10 black females were sexually active by age 16 and more than 8 out of 10 were sexually active by age 20. In contrast, only 1 out of 10 white and Hispanic females were sexually active by age 16 and 7 out of 10 were sexually active by age 20.

In general, males were sexually active at younger ages than females, and blacks were sexually active at younger ages than whites or Hispanics.

TABLE 1.5 Cumulative Percentage Of Women And Men Under 20 Who Ever Had Intercourse, By Age, Race And Study, United States, 1938 to 1984

			Females		Males	
Study	Year	Age	White	Black	White	Black
Kinsey, Pomeroy	1938-50	13	1	--	14.8	--
& Martin, 1948		14	2	--	27.8	--
Kinsey, Pomeroy,		15	3	--	38.8	--
Martin & Gebhard,		16	7	--	51.6	--
1953, U.S.		17	--	--	61.3	--
		18	--	--	68.2	--
		19	--	--	71.5	--
		20	20	--	73.1	--
Vener & Stewart,	1970	13	10	--	24	--
1974; Michigan,		14	10	--	21	--
School B		15	13	--	26	--
Sample,		16	23	--	31	--
Tables 4 & 5		17+	27	--	38	--
		TOTAL	16	--	28	--
	1973	13	10	--	28	--
		14	17	--	32	--
		15	24	--	38	--
		16	31	--	38	--
		17+	35	--	34	--
		TOTAL	22	--	33	--
Miller & Simon	1971	14-15	5.3	--	7.8	--
1974, Illinois		16-17	21.7	--	20.9	--
Table 3		TOTAL	13.0	--	14.0	--
Sorenson, 1973	1972	13-15	30		44	
Table 404, U.S.		16-19	57		72	
		TOTAL	45		59	
Simon, Berger &	1967	lt 18	7	--	25	--
Gaznon, 1972		18	19	--	36	--
Table III (College		19	30	--	63	--
Youth, U.S.)						
Jessor & Jessor	1972	Grade 10	26	--	21	--
1975, Colorado		11	40	--	28	--
Table 1		12	55	--	33	--
Udry, 1980						
Raleigh, NC	1978	13	6.1	35.0	27.0	69.8
Tallahassee, FL	1980	14	11.0	39.3	28.8	75.9
Zabin el al, 1984	1981-82	lt 16	34.8	54.0	65.9	83.3
Inner city Baltimore,		16+	59.9	80.3	76.8	93.1

Source: Refer to references at the end of text.

TABLE 1.5

Table 1.5 presents cumulative percentage distributions of women and men under age 20 who ever had intercourse by age, race and study for the United States from 1938 to 1964. This table shows both the trends over time in adolescent sexual activity and variations and consistencies in sample estimates.

TABLE 1.6 Percent of Sexually Experienced Never-Married Women Aged 15-19 Who Had Intercourse Only Once, by Age and Race, 1976

		Race			
		White		Black	
Age	All	%	N	%	N
15-19	14.8	14.3	379	12.7	410
15-17	19.9	18.4	206	18.4	217
18-19	8.6	9.3	173	6.2	193

Source: M. Zelnik and J.T. Kantner, "Sexual and Contraceptive Experience of Young Unmarried Women in the United States 1976 and 1971." Family Planning Perspectives 9, 1977. Reprinted by permission.

TABLE 1.6

Table 1.6 shows the percent of a sample of sexually experienced never-married women aged 15 to 19 in 1976 who had only had sexual intercourse once. Data are from the 1976 National Survey of Young Women (NSYW). Among sexually experienced never-married 15- to 19-year-old women, nearly 15 percent had sexual intercourse only once. About 20 percent of women aged 15 to 17 and fewer than 10 percent of women ages 18 to 19 reported having had intercourse only one time. There were no substantial differences by race.

TABLE 1.7 Frequency Of Sexual Intercourse Among Unmarried Females 15 To 24 Who Ever Had Intercourse By Race, 1982 National Survey Of Family Growth

Frequency of Intercourse	Age			
	15-17	18-19	15-19	20-24
All Races*				
Total ever having intercourse	100.0% (N=295)	100.0% (N=473)	100.0% (N=768)	100.0% (N=626)
No intercourse in last 3 months	18.3	17.9	18.1	24.3
Once a month	20.7	13.5	16.4	14.2
2-3 times a month	27.9	23.0	25.0	22.3
Once a week	21.4	20.6	20.9	18.5
More than twice per week	9.8	20.7	16.3	19.3
Daily	1.9	4.3	3.3	1.4
White				
Total ever having intercourse	100.0% (N=146)	100.0% (N=175)	100.0% (N=321)	100.0% (N=367)
No intercourse in last 3 months	21.0	20.5	20.7	27.8
Once a month	14.5	11.1	12.4	14.5
2-3 times a month	29.2	20.8	24.1	20.5
Once a week	23.2	20.7	21.6	17.0
More than twice per week	10.8	22.0	17.6	19.3
Daily	1.3	4.9	3.6	0.9
Black				
Total ever having intercourse	100.0% (N=146)	100.0% (N=291)	100.0% (N=437)	100.0% (N=250)
No intercourse in last 3 months	11.8	7.5	9.5	15.0
Once a month	39.5	23.0	30.8	12.6
2-3 times a month	24.9	29.4	27.2	29.8
Once a week	13.3	21.0	17.4	21.3
More than twice per week	7.2	16.9	12.3	18.8
Daily	3.3	2.2	2.7	2.5

*Includes Blacks, White and other. Other category too small to percentage.

Source: Special Tabulations from the 1982 National Survey of Family Growth, Cycle III, conducted by the National Center for Health Statistics, DHHS.

TABLE 1.7

Table 1.7 presents the percentage distributions of unmarried females aged 15 to 24 who ever had sexual intercourse by race according to frequency of intercourse. These data are from the 1982 National Survey of Family Growth. (NSFG)

Overall, 18.1 percent of sexually experienced female teenagers reported that they had not had intercourse in the three months prior to the interview, 20.7 percent of whites and 9.5 percent of blacks. The young teenagers, aged 15 to 17, were somewhat less likely to have had sexual intercourse twice per week or more frequently than older teenagers.

TABLE 1.8 Distribution (in percentages) Of Total Number Of Premarital Sexual Partners, By Race: 1971, 1976 And 1979 - Sexually Experienced Females Aged 15 to 19, Metropolitan U.S.

	Sexually Experienced Females Aged 15-19								
	1971			1976			1979		
No. Of Partners*	Total (n=919)	White (n=431)	Black (n=488)	Total (n=714)	White (n=344)	Black (n=370)	Total (n=933)	White (n=476)	Black (n=457)
1	61.7	61.8	61.4	52.5	56.2	42.8	48.9	51.1	40.9
2-3	24.6	23.0	29.5	27.7	23.0	40.0	35.1	33.0	42.7
4-5	6.8	7.4	5.1	9.1	8.2	11.6	7.9	7.0	11.4
6 or more	6.9	7.8	4.0	10.7	12.6	5.6	8.1	8.9	5.0
Mean	n/a	n/a	n/a	2.9	3.0	2.4	2.6	2.7	2.5

*In the 1971 survey these precoded categories were used; in the 1976 and 1979 surveys individual responses were recoded.

n/a: Not available.

Source: M. Zelnik, "Sexual Activity Among Adolescents: Perspective of a Decade," In E.R. McAnarey (Ed.), Premature Adolescent Pregnancy and Parenthood. New York: Grune and Stratton, 1983. Reprinted by permission.

TABLE 1.8

The percentage distribution of a sample of women by race and by total number of premarital sexual partners as of the survey date is shown for 1971, 1976 and 1979 in Table 1.8. The percent of women who had had only one premarital sexual partner was lower in 1979 than in 1976 or 1971, 49 compared to 53 and 62 percent respectively. The largest difference was for black women. In 1971, 60 percent of the black women had had only one premarital sexual partner, while in 1979 about 40 percent of the black women had had only one premarital sexual partner. There was about an 11 percent age point decline in the number of white women who had had one partner in 1971 compared to 1979, 62 versus 51 percent. Although in all years white teenagers were more likely than black teenagers to have had only one nonmarital sexual partner, they were slightly more likely than blacks to have had 6 or more such partners.

TABLE 1.9 Percentage Distribution Of Women Aged 15-19 And Of Men Aged 17-21, By Relationship With Their First Sexual Partner, According To Race, 1979, Metropolitan U.S.

Relationship With First Partner	Women			Men		
	Total (N=936)	White (N=478)	Black (N=458)	Total (N=670)	White (N=396)	Black (N=274)
Engaged	9.3	9.6	8.2	0.6	0.5	1.0
Going steady	55.2	57.6	46.5	36.5	39.2	21.9
Dating	24.4	22.2	32.6	20.0	20.2	19.0
Friends	6.7	6.0	9.4	33.7	30.2	52.4
Recently met	4.4	4.6	3.3	9.3	9.9	5.7
Total	100.0	100.0	100.0	100.0	100.0	100.0

Source: M. Zelnik and F.K. Shah, "First Intercourse Among Young Americans," Family Planning Perspectives, 15 (2) (March/April), 1983. Reprinted by permission.

TABLE 1.9

Table 1.9 shows the percentage distribution of women aged 15 to 19 and of men aged 17 to 21 by their relationship with their first sexual partner by race. Data are from the National Survey of Young Women (NSYW) for metropolitan areas only in 1979.

Among the women, over 85 percent of the white and black women were engaged, going steady, or dating their first sexual partners. Only 4.6 percent of the white women and 3.3 percent of the black women had recently met their first sexual partners. Among males, however, 40 percent of the white men and 58 percent of the black men said that their first sexual partners were friends or someone they had just recently met.

TABLE 1.9

Table 1.9 shows the percentage distribution of women aged 15 to 19 and of men aged 17 to 21 by their relationship with their first sexual partner by race. Data are from the National Survey of Young Women (NSYW) for metropolitan areas only in 1979.

Among the women, over 85 percent of the white and black women were engaged, going steady, or dating their first sexual partners. Only 4.6 percent of the white women and 3.3 percent of the black women had recently met their first sexual partners. Among males, however, 40 percent of the white men and 58 percent of the black men said that their first sexual partners were friends or someone they had just recently met.

TABLE 1.10

Table 1.10 shows the percentage distribution of women aged 15 to 19 and of men aged 17 to 21 by relationship with their first sexual partner according to age at first intercourse. Data are from the National Survey of Young Women (NSYW) for metropolitan areas only in 1979.

Among women, teenagers who were younger at first intercourse (less than 17 years) were more likely to have recently met and less likely to be engaged to their first partner than teenage women who had first intercourse at age 18 or 19. Among males, however, those who first had sexual intercourse at age 18 to 21 were more likely to have recently met their first partner than males who first had intercourse under age 18.

TABLE 1.11 Percentage Distribution Of Locale Of First Premarital Intercourse, Women Aged 15-19, By Race, 1976 And 1979, Metropolitan U.S.

Locale	1976			1979		
	Total (N=713)	White (N=345)	Black (N=368)	Total (N=923)	White (N=469)	Black (N=454)
Respondent's home	17.6	16.2	21.2	18.5	17.9	20.7
Partner's home	43.5	43.8	43.1	49.2	48.4	51.7
Home of relative/friend	21.1	21.5	20.2	12.3	12.6	11.5
Motel/hotel	5.5	3.3	11.5	4.2	2.2	11.7
Car	7.1	8.9	2.0	8.9	10.6	2.7
Elsewhere	5.2	6.3	2.0	6.9	8.3	1.7

Source: M. Zelnik, "Sexual Activity Among Adolescents: Perspective of a Decade," In E.R. McAnarey (Ed.), Premature Adolescent Pregnancy and Parenthood. New York: Grune and Stratton, 1983. Reprinted by permission.

TABLE 1.11

Table 1.11 shows the percentage distribution of the location of first nonmarital intercourse for women aged 15 to 19 by race. The data are from the National Survey of Young Women (NSYW) for 1976 and 1979, metropolitan areas only.

For the majority, over three-quarters, in both 1976 and 1979, of all the women aged 15-19 who had a first premarital intercourse, the location was the home of the respondent, the partner or a friend or relative. In both years, black women were more likely than white women to first have sexual intercourse in a motel/hotel. For white women the location of first premarital intercourse was more likely to be a car or elsewhere than for black women. The partner's home was twice as likely to be the location of first intercourse as the young women's home.

TABLE 1.12 Estimated Cummulative Percent Ever Experiencing Sexual Intercourse By Single Year of Age, Race, Ethnicity[1] And Mother's Education, 1983, National Longitudinal Survey of Youth

	Males			Females		
	Respondent's Mother's Education[2]					
Age*	<HS	= HS	>HS	<HS	= HS	>HS
Total Sample						
15	23.9	13.7	12.0	7.3	4.7	3.3
16	38.0	24.8	23.0	16.9	10.2	10.4
17	57.9	43.8	40.6	34.6	23.7	21.4
18	72.4	61.8	55.6	53.7	40.5	34.1
19	83.5	77.6	68.7	71.8	61.4	50.5
20	87.6	82.8	76.5	81.3	73.4	60.8
N	1808	1878	790	1975	1791	756
Whites						
15	18.5	9.9	9.7	6.3	4.5	3.2
16	31.2	20.4	20.6	15.9	9.2	10.5
17	52.8	40.0	37.2	33.6	22.6	20.2
18	68.6	58.8	52.9	53.5	39.1	31.9
19	81.3	75.8	66.4	72.4	59.9	48.5
20	85.7	91.5	74.9	82.0	72.4	59.0
N	814	1359	592	883	1288	577
Blacks						
15	42.8	43.7	12.0	6.8		
16	62.7	58.0	23.2	16.1		
17	79.3	76.3	44.0	33.8		
18	87.7	85.1	63.2	53.9		
19	93.0	92.5	80.1	72.0		
20	94.5	94.0	87.2	80.6		
N	541	525	595	499		
Hispanics						
15	20.8	16.1	4.8	2.9		
16	32.2	29.0	12.2	8.7		
17	49.6	46.7	24.3	19.4		
18	66.9	65.5	39.0	38.9		
19	79.3	76.5	55.8	62.0		
20	86.0	79.9	68.0	70.8		
N	453	192	496	183		

Note: Sample is limited to respondents age 20 and over at 1983 survey date.

*Percentages refer to birthday for specified ages, e.g., 15 means by 15th birthday or end of age 14.

[1] Hispanic persons may be of any race.
[2] Education is defined as less than High School, completing High School or more than High School (not available for Blacks and Hispanics).

Source: Special Tabulations from the 1983 National Longitudinal Survey of Youth, Center for Human Resource Research, Ohio State University.

TABLE 1.12

Table 1.12 shows cumulative estimates of sexual activity by single year of age and mother's education in 1983 for a national sample of youths. Data are from the National Longitudinal Survey of Youth (NLS).

In general, the lower the mother's educational level, the lower the respondent's age at becoming sexually active. For the total sample, more than half (57.9 percent) of the males whose mothers had less than high school educations and about two fifths of the males whose mothers had a high school education or more than a high school education were sexually active by age 17 (43.8 and 40.6 percent).

Slightly over a third of the females whose mothers had less than high school educations (34.6 percent) and less than one quarter of the females whose mothers had a high school education or more (23.7 and 21.4 percent) were sexually active by age 17.

Black males were more likely to be sexually active by age 20 than whites and Hispanics and, Hispanic males were as likely to be as sexually active white males by age 20, regardless of mother's education. Black females were more likely to be sexually active by age 20 than whites and Hispanics regardless of mother's education.

TABLE 1.13 Cumulative Sexual Activity By Single Year Of Age And By Drop Out Rate Of Respondent's High School, 1979 From National Longitudinal Survey Of Youth

	Drop-Out Rate of Respondent's High School, 1979			
	Males		Females	
Age*	LO (<10%)	HI (10%+)	LO (<10%)	HI (10%+)
Total Sample				
15	10.7	18.8	3.4	5.1
16	21.5	31.5	9.2	12.8
17	40.7	50.4	20.6	28.4
18	59.1	65.8	36.5	45.1
19	73.4	79.4	56.5	64.6
20	81.0	82.8	68.3	75.4
N	1387	1454	1441	1523
Whites				
15	8.4	13.5	3.2	4.2
16	17.9	26.1	8.9	11.5
17	37.3	45.4	19.9	26.1
18	56.5	61.9	35.4	41.9
19	71.7	77.4	55.5	61.9
20	79.7	80.7	67.5	73.8
N	998	762	1053	806
Blacks				
15	35.6	45.2	6.4	8.6
16	58.3	59.3	13.6	18.5
17	73.9	77.0	28.1	40.6
18	83.9	86.1	48.8	62.3
19	91.4	92.1	68.1	80.0
20	92.8	94.4	78.5	86.3
N	268	411	268	447
Hispanics				
15	9.8	19.2	.4	5.9
16	26.6	29.6	5.5	12.6
17	47.5	46.8	17.9	23.1
18	64.7	63.4	34.3	36.4
19	76.1	74.4	52.3	55.4
20	84.2	80.3	63.5	66.3
N	121	281	120	270

Note: Sample is limited to respondents age 20 and over at 1983 survey date.

*Percentages refer to birthday for specified ages, e.g., 15 means by 15th birthday or end of age 14.

[1]Hispanic Persons may be of any race.

Source: Special Tabulations from the 1983 National Longitudinal Survey of Youth, Center for Human Resource Research, Ohio State University.

TABLE 1.13

Table 1.13 presents data from the National Longitudinal Survey of Youth on cumulative sexual activity by single year of age and the drop out rate in the respondent's high school.

In general, the percent sexually active by age 20 was higher among respondents who attended schools with high drop-out rates (greater than 10 percent) compared to respondents who attended schools with low drop-out rates (10 percent or lower). Again, the incidence of sexual activity was greater among black males and females regardless of the drop-out rate in the respondent's high school.

It should be noted that high school drop-out rates may be a consequence of levels of sexual activity as well as a measure of the community context.

II. CONTRACEPTIVE USE AMONG ADOLESCENTS

This section presents information on contraceptive use among U.S. adolescents. Most of the available data are on females, but data from the National Surveys of Young Women and Men (NSYW/M) on male contraceptive use are presented. Data from the 1982 NSFG are also presented in this section.

Among limitations of the data on contraceptive use are the lack of information on males, and the lack of standardization of contraceptive categories across surveys. In the tables that follow, data on contraceptive use are presented for sexually active men and women by marital status, timing of use (i.e., just intercourse, most recent intercourse, currently).

TABLE 2.1 Percentage Distribution Of Sexually Active Women Aged 15-19, By Contraceptive-Use Status, According To Race, 1976, 1979, 1982

Contraceptive-Use Status	1982[a]			1979[b,c]			1976[b,c]		
	Total* (N=945)	White (N=579)	Black (N=342)	Total (N=937)	White (N=478)	Black (N=459)	Total (N=724)	White (N=349)	Black (N=375)
Always used	48.2	52.1	36.0	34.2	35.0	31.2	28.7	28.9	28.0
Used at first intercourse but not always				14.7	16.1	9.7	9.5	10.1	8.1
Did not use at 1st intercourse but used at some time	37.2	34.9	43.7	24.5	24.9	23.3	26.3	28.6	20.2
Never used	14.6	13.0	20.3	26.6	24.0	35.9	35.5	32.4	43.7
Total	100.0	100.0	100.0	100.0	100.0	100.0	100.0	100.0	100.0

[a] All women 15-19 sexually active, including married women.
[b] Premaritally sexually active women 15-19; contraceptive use refers to use prior to pregnancy, marriage or time of survey, whichever event was earlier.
[c] Metropolitan U.S. only.

*Includes races other than Black and White.

Source: Unpublished Tabulations from the 1982 National Survey of Family Growth. Zelnik and Kanter, "Sexual Activity, Contraceptive Use and Pregnancy Among Metropolitan-Area Teenagers", 1971-1976, "Family Planning Perspectives," Vol. 12, Sept. - Oct. 1980.

TABLE 2.1

Table 2.1 displays the percentage distribution of premaritally sexually active females aged 15 to 19 in 1976, 1979, and 1982 by contraceptive-use status according to race. Data are from the National Surveys of Young Women (NSYW) for 1976 and 1979 and from the National Survey of Family Growth (NSFG) for 1982. Overall, the proportion of premaritally sexually active females who always used a contraceptive and who used a contraceptive at some time was higher in 1979 than in 1976. In 1976, 29 percent of the sample reported that they always used a contraceptive and about 36 percent reported that they used a contraceptive at some time. In 1979, 34 percent of the premaritally sexually active females said they always used a contraceptive and about 40 said they used a contraceptive at least some of the time.

White premaritally sexual active teenage females were more likely to have used a contraceptive than blacks in both 1976 and 1979. The proportion of those never using a contraceptive was somewhat lower in 1979 than in 1976 for both races. Even in 1979, though, a quarter of the young women had never used a method of birth control, about 36 percent of the black females and nearly a quarter of the white females. In 1976, over 40 percent of the sexually active black female teenagers and about one-third of the whites had never used a contraceptive before marriage.

The 1982 data include only women aged 15 to 19 who did not always use contraception. Among these women, 48.2 percent used at first intercourse, 52.1 percent of the white women and 36.0 percent of the black women. A lower proportion of women had never used a contraceptive method in 1982 compared to 1976, regardless of race. Only 14.6 percent of all sexually active 15- to 19-year old women had never used any method in 1982, 12 percentage points lower than in 1979.

TABLE 2.2 Percent Of Women Aged 15-44 Who Used A Contraceptive Method At First Intercourse And Percent Distribution Of Women Who Used A Method, By Type Of Method, 1982 National Survey Of Family Growth

Characteristics	Percent Who Used a Method At First Intercourse	Percent Distribution of Those Using Contraception, by Method						
		Pill	IUD	Diaphragm	Condom	Rhythm	Withdrawal	Other
Total, 15-44	44.5	28.2	0.5	1.9	38.5	5.3	19.1	6.5
15-19	48.2	17.3	0.1	0.2	46.6	4.3	27.2	4.5
15-17	40.2	14.6	0.2	--	51.4	7.6	24.7	1.5
20-44	44.1	29.4	0.6	2.1	37.6	5.4	18.1	6.7

Source: Pratt et al. "Understanding U.S. Fertility," Population Bulletin, Volume 39 No. 5, December 1984. Reprinted by permission.

TABLE 2.2

The percent of women of all ages who used a contraceptive at first intercourse by age and method is shown in Table 2.2. Data are from the 1982 National Survey of Family Growth. (NSFG)

Among all women aged 15 to 44 in 1982, slightly less than one-half used a contraceptive method at first intercourse. For the older women in the sample who used a method, the most commonly used methods at first intercourse were the condom (37.6 percent), the pill (29.4 percent) and withdrawal (18.1 percent). Women currently aged 15 to 17 were the least likely to have used a method at first intercourse, all of them having been under 18 when they initiated coitus. Those women aged 15-19 in 1982 who used any method were most likely to have used the condom (46.6 percent), withdrawal (24.7 percent) and the pill (17.3 percent). The table show that less than half of all women used contraceptives at first intercourse, regardless of current age. The largest difference was between those who had first intercourse before age 18 or at age 18 or older.

TABLE 2.3 Percentage Distribution Of Sexually Experienced Women Aged 15-19 And Men Aged 17-21, By Type Of Contraceptive Method Used At First Intercourse; Percentage Distribution Of Those Using A Method, By Type Of Method; According To Race And Planning Status Of First Intercourse, 1979, Metropolitan U.S.

Type of Method Used at First Intercourse	Women Total Planned	Women Total Unplanned	Women White Planned	Women White Unplanned	Women Black Planned	Women Black Unplanned	Men Total Planned	Men Total Unplanned	Men White Planned	Men White Unplanned	Men Black Planned	Men Black Unplanned
All respondents	(N=166)	(N=767)	(N=78)	(N=399)	(N=88)	(N=368)	(N=162)	(N=495)	(N=98)	(N=292)	(N=64)	(N=203)
Female prescription	16.7	8.3	14.3	6.5	24.7	14.9	10.1	9.6	10.1	9.9	10.1	8.1
Female non-prescription	4.9	2.9	3.8	2.7	8.3	3.6	4.5	4.5	4.7	4.6	3.2	3.4
Male	50.0	33.1	58.6	36.8	21.3	19.4	36.3	27.8	37.0	29.6	32.8	18.0
Condom	(32.1)	(14.8)	(35.6)	(14.7)	(20.5)	(15.2)	(24.4)	(15.5)	(25.2)	(16.4)	(20.7)	(10.4)
Withdrawal	(17.9)	(18.3)	(23.0)	(22.1)	(0.8)	(4.2)	(11.9)	(12.3)	(11.8)	(13.2)	(12.1)	(7.6)
None	28.4	55.7	23.3	54.0	45.7	62.1	49.1	58.1	48.2	55.9	53.9	70.5
All users	(N=106)	(N=319)	(N=59)	(N=179)	(N=47)	(N=140)	(N=78)	(N=200)	(N=52)	(N=135)	(N=26)	(N=65)
Female prescription	23.4	18.7	18.7	14.1	45.5	39.4	19.8	23.0	19.5	22.4	21.9	27.4
Female non-prescription	6.7	6.6	5.0	5.9	15.2	9.4	8.8	10.6	9.0	10.6	7.0	11.6
Male	69.9	74.7	76.3	80.0	39.3	51.2	71.4	66.4	71.5	67.0	71.1	61.0
Total	100.0	100.0	100.0	100.0	100.0	100.0	100.0	100.0	100.0	100.0	100.0	100.0

Source: Special tabulations from the 1982 National Survey of Family Growth, Cycle III, conducted by the National Center for Health Statistics, DHHS; M. Zelnik and F.K. Shah, "First Intercourse Among Young Americans," Family Planning Perspectives, 15 (a) March/April, 1983.

TABLE 2.3

Table 2.3 shows the percentage distribution of sexually experienced women aged 15 to 19 and men aged 17 to 21 by the type of contraceptive method used at first intercourse and the percentage distribution for those using a method by type of method according to race and planning status of first intercourse for 1979. Data are from the National Survey of Young Women (NSYW).

Among women and men, those who planned first intercourse were more likely to have used contraception than those who did not plan first intercourse. Of the women who used a method at first intercourse, the planners were more likely than those who did not plan to use a female prescription method while male planners were more likely than those who did not plan to use a male contraceptive method. Black women were more likely than other young men and women to rely on a female prescription method.

TABLE 2.4 Percentage Distribution Of Sexually Experienced Women Aged 15-19 By Type of Contraceptive Method Used At First Intercourse; Percentage Distribution Of Those Using A Method, By Type Of Method; According To Race, 1982 National Survey Of Family Growth

Type of Method Used at First Intercourse	Percent Using		
	Total*	White	Black
All Respondents:	(N=945)	(N=579)	(N=342)
Female prescription	8.4	8.0	10.6
Female nonprescription	4.3	4.9	1.9
Male	35.6	39.1	23.4
Condom	22.5	23.6	18.8
Withdrawal	13.1	15.5	4.6
None	51.8	47.9	64.0
Users only:			
Female prescription	17.4	15.4	29.6
Female nonprescription	8.9	9.4	5.4
Male	73.8	75.1	65.0
Condom	46.6	45.3	52.1
Withdrawal	27.2	29.8	12.9

*Includes races other than white and black.

Source: See Table 2.3

TABLE 2.4

Table 2.4 shows the percentage distribution of sexually experienced women aged 15 to 19 by type of contraceptive method used at first intercourse and the percentage of those using a method, by type of method, according to race. Data are from the National Survey of Family Growth (NSFG).

Black women aged 15 to 19 were more likely than white women to have used no method at first intercourse. Among the users, black females were more likely to have used a female prescription method and less likely to have used withdrawal than white women.

TABLE 2.5 Percentage Distribution Of Sexually Experienced Women Aged 15-19 And Men Aged 17-21 Who Did Not Use A Contraceptive Method At First Intercourse, By Reason Reported For Not Having Used A Method, According To Planning Status Of First Intercourse And Race, 1979, Metropolitan U.S.

Reason for Non-use	Women				Men			
	Planned	Unplanned			Planned	Unplanned		
	Total (N=56)	Total (N=424)	White (N=211)	Black (N=213)	Total (N=71)	Total (N=263)	White (N=40)	Black (N=123)
Wanted pregnancy or didn't care	3.5	4.6	4.7	4.5	4.9	1.8	1.8	1.4
Didn't want to use contraceptives[a]	31.2	8.0	5.3	17.0	25.6	15.3	13.4	24.1
Didn't know about contraception	19.8	12.4	9.2	22.8	19.3	19.9	16.1	36.6
Didn't think about using contraceptives	13.5	24.3	26.8	16.3	15.7	15.4	17.5	5.8
Intercourse was not planned	0.0	31.8	34.1	24.1	0.0	23.6	26.5	10.5
Contraception was not available	14.4	12.9	14.4	7.8	25.7	20.2	22.0	12.5
Thought pregnancy was impossible	16.2	5.0	4.7	5.6	8.5	3.2	2.7	5.7
Other	1.4	1.0	0.8	1.9	0.3	0.6	0.0	3.4
Total	100.0	100.0	100.0	100.0	100.0	100.0	100.0	100.0

Note: Too few teenagers planned their first intercourse to allow for separate analysis by race.

[a] Category includes partner's objection to the use of contraceptives.

Source: See Table 2.3

TABLE 2.5

Table 2.5 shows the percentage distribution of sexually experienced women aged 15 to 19 and men aged 17 to 21 who did not use a contraceptive method at first intercourse by reason reported for not having used a contraceptive method, according to planning status of first intercourse and race. The data are from the 1979 National Survey of Young Women (NSYW) for metropolitan areas only.

For both males and females regardless of whether they planned first intercourse, less than 5 percent of those not using contraception at first intercourse reported that they wanted to become pregnant or did not care if a pregnancy occurred. Among those who planned first intercourse and did not use contraception, 16.2 percent of the women and 8.5 percent of the men, thought pregnancy was impossible, and 31.2 percent of the women and 25.6 percent of the men said they did not want to use contraception. Among those who did not plan first intercourse, white men and women were more likely than blacks to indicate that contraception was not available and more black men and women indicated that they did not know about contraception than white men and women.

TABLE 2.6 Percent Of Sexually Active Unmarried Women Under Age 20 By Timing Of First Contraception And Age At First Intercourse, According To Race, 1982, National Survey Of Family Growth*

Months Since First Intercourse	All Races**			White			Black		
	<15	15-17	18-19	<15	15-17	18-19	<15	15-17	18-19
	(N=167)	(N=293)	(N=73)	(N=38)	(N=111)	(N=42)	(N=127)	(N=179)	(N=30)
0-1	22.6	36.9	53.3	24.4	41.8	55.6	22.9	28.3	43.6
1-3	14.8	13.5	20.1	20.2	14.2	21.9	10.4	11.7	12.4
4-6	12.5	5.0	8.6	12.1	6.2	8.6	14.3	2.9	8.6
7-12	8.0	10.0	2.7	7.6	9.5	1.4	9.2	10.7	8.5
More than 12	42.2	34.6	15.3	35.8	28.2	12.4	43.2	46.4	26.9

*Includes only women who did not use a method at first intercourse but have ever used a method.

**Includes races other than black and white.

Source: Special tabulations from the 1982 National Survey of Family Growth, Cycle III, conducted by the National Center for Health Statistics.

TABLE 2.6

The percentage distribution of sexually active unmarried women under age 20 by the timing of first contraception and age at first intercourse according to race is shown in Table 2.6. The data are from the 1982 National Survey of Family Growth (NSFG), and include only women who did not use contraceptives at first intercourse but used it at sometime after first intercourse.

The data indicate that younger teenage women (under age 15 and aged 15 to 17) were more likely than older teenagers to delay more than 12 months after first intercourse to begin using contraceptives. This was true regardless of race, but black teenagers were especially likely to delay using contraception. Only among whites aged 18 and 19 does a majority initiate contraceptive use within the first or second month after initiating sexual activity.

TABLE 2.7 Number of Women Aged 15-44 Exposed To The Risk Of Unintended Pregnancy,[a] And Percentage Currently Practicing Contraception, By Marital Status, by Age, 1982 National Survey Of Family Growth

	Number (in 1,000s)				Percentage Using Contraception			
Age	Total	Never Married	Currently Married	Widowed, Divorced or Separated	Total	Never Married	Currently Married	Widowed, Divorced or Separated
All women	33,481	8,664	20,534	4,284	88.1	77.6	93.4	82.7
15-24	10,045	6,145	3,318	583	81.6	75.3	92.8	84.3
15-19	3,244	2,853	361	b	71.0	68.6	90.0	b
20-24	6,801	3,291	2,957	553	86.6	81.0	93.1	85.2
25-34	14,004	}	9,549	2,191	90.9	}	94.2	83.9
35-44	9,432	9,432	7,667	1,509	90.9	83.5	92.8	83.1

[a]Includes women practicing contraception and those not practicing contraception who had sexual intercourse in the last three months and were not pregnant, postpartum, seeking pregnancy, or noncontraceptively sterile.
[b]Number or percentage based on less than 20 cases.

Source: C.A. Bachrach, "Contraceptive Practice Among American Women, 1973-1982", *Family Planning Perspectives*, (16) 6 (Nov./Dec.) 1984. Reprinted by permission.

TABLE 2.7

Table 2.7 shows the estimated number of women aged 15 to 44 exposed to the risk of unintended pregnancy and the percentage currently practicing contraception, by marital status and age. Data are from the 1982 National Survey of Family Growth (NSFG). Women exposed to the risk of an unintended pregnancy includes women practicing contraception and those not practicing contraception who had sexual intercourse in the last three months and were not pregnant, post partum, seeking pregnancy or non-contraceptively sterile.

These data indicate that among women aged 15 to 44 exposed to the risk of an unintended pregnancy, never-married women aged 15 to 19 were the least likely to be currently using contraception, whereas there were no differences among married women.

TABLE 2.3: Number Of Never Married Women 15-44 Years Of Age Who Were Exposed To The Risk Of An Unintended Pregnancy, And Percent Using A Method Of Contraception, By Race And Age, And Percent Distribution Of Contraceptors By Method Of Contraception, According To Race And Age: United States, 1982 (preliminary data based on a sample of the household population of the coterminous United States)

	All Races[3]						White						Black				
	15-44	15-19	15-17	18-19	20-24	20-44	15-44	15-19	15-17	18-19	20-24	20-44	15-44	15-19	15-17	18-19	20-24
No. Exposed[1]	8,727	2,872	1,081		3,291	5,885	6,372	2,188	803			4,184	2,098	618	253		1,480
Percent Using a Method	76.1	67.6	60.0		81.0	80.3	77.4	69.0	60.2			81.8	73.0	63.9	58.7		76.9
Method Chosen by Users:																	
Pill	53.2	62.3	63.7		56.1	49.5	51.6	59.6	62.4			48.1	58.9	71.4	65.1		54.6
IUD	5.0	0.9*	1.3*		4.9*	6.7	3.7*	0.1*	0.3*			5.4*	8.0*	4.2*	4.5*		9.4
Diaphragm	13.7	6.4	3.6		13.8	16.6	17.1	7.8	4.4			21.2	2.6	2.0	1.5		2.9
Condom	11.8	22.2	25.0		8.3	7.5	13.0	24.7	28.6			7.9	7.9	13.0	14.5		6.1
Sterilization	5.1	0.4*	--		3.8*	7.0	3.1*	0.6*	--			4.2*	12.1	--	--		16.3
Other Methods[2]	11.2	7.8*	6.4*		13.0*	12.7*	11.4	7.3	4.2*			13.2*	10.4*	9.5*	14.3*		10.7
Total	100.0	100.0	100.0		100.0	100.0	100.0	100.0	100.0			100.0	100.0	100.0	100.0		100.7

[1]Includes women using contraception and those not using contraception who had sexual intercourse in the last 3 months and were not pregnant, post partum, seeking pregnancy, or noncontraceptively sterile.
[2]Includes foam, periodic abstinence, withdrawal, douche, suppositories, and other methods.
[3]Includes white, black, and other races.

*Figure does not meet standards of reliability or precision (30 percent or more relative standard error)

Source: C. A. Bachrach and W.D. Mosher: "Use of Contraception in the United States, 1982." National Center for Health Statistics, Advance Data from Vital and Health Statistics, No. 102, December 4, 1984; C.A. Bachrach, "Contraceptive Practice Among American Women, 1973-1982," Family Planning Perspectives (Nov./Dec.): 253-259, 1984.

TABLE 2.8

Table 2.8 shows the number of never-married women exposed to an unintended pregnancy and the percent who used any contraceptive method by age and race. For women using any method, the percentage distribution of type of contraceptive method is presented by age and race for 1982.

Among all never-married women aged 15 to 44 exposed to an unintended pregnancy, 3 out of every 4 were using a method of birth control-- 77 percent of the white women and 73 percent of the black women. The pill was the most commonly used method by all exposed women.

Among teenage women aged 15 to 19, 69 percent of the exposed white women and 64 percent of exposed black women used a method. Women aged 15 to 19 who were exposed to an unintended pregnancy and who were using contraception were more likely to use the pill then older women, 71 percent of black teens and 60 percent of white teens, compared to 55 and 48 percent of older women respectively.

TABLE 2.9 Number And Percentage Distribution Of Hispanic And Non-Hispanic Women Aged 15 To 19 (All Marital Statuses) Currently Exposed To The Risk Of Unintended Pregnancy By Current Contraceptive Status, 1982 National Survey of Family Growth.

	Total	Hispanic	Non-Hispanic Black	Non-Hispanic White & Other
No. currently exposed (in 1,000s)	3244	290	630	2,324
Total	100	100	100	100
Using contraception	71	68	66	73
No contraception	29	32	35	27
<u>Users Only</u>				
No.	2302	197	413	1692
Total	100	100	100	100
Pill	64	63	70	63
IUD, sterilization	2	9	5	0
Condom	21	15	13	23
Diaphragm	6	5	2	7
Other	8	8	10	7

Source: A. Torres and S. Singh, Hispanic Adolescents and Contraception: An Analyses of Data from the 1982 National Survey of Family Growth Paper presented at the Annual Meeting of the APHA, 1985.

TABLE 2.9

Table 2.9 presents the estimated number and percentage distribution of Hispanic and non-Hispanic women aged 15 to 19 currently exposed to the risk of an unintended pregnancy by current contraceptive use status. These data are from the 1982 National Survey of Family Growth (NSFG), and they are categorized by ethnicity, not by race. Thus, persons of Hispanic origin may be black or white, but black, white and other persons cannot be of Hispanic origin. The definition of exposure to the risk of an unintended pregnancy is the same as that provided for Table 1.7.

Among Hispanic women aged 15 to 19 exposed to the risk of an unintended pregnancy, 68 percent were using some form of contraception. This proportion is slightly higher than for non-hispanic blacks and slightly lower than for non-Hispanic whites and others, but differences are very small.

Hispanic women aged 15 to 19 exposed to the risk of an unintended pregnancy and using contraception were as likely as non-Hispanic whites and others to use the pill and more likely than non-Hispanic blacks and non-Hispanic whites and others to use the IUD or sterilization.

TABLE 2.10 Percent Of Never-Married Women Aged 15-19 Who Correctly Perceived The Time Of Greatest Pregnancy Risk Within The Menstrual Cycle, By Age, Race And Sexual Experience, 1976 And 1971

	Race and Sexual Experience														
	All			White						Black					
				Total		Experi-enced		Not Ex-perienced		Total		Experi-enced		Not Ex-perienced	
Age	Total	Experi-enced	Not ex-perienced	%	N	%	N	%	N	%	N	%	N	%	N
1976															
15-19	40.6	47.3	36.9	43.9	1,194	53.2	365	39.8	829	23.5	646	24.0	405	22.8	241
15	29.5	33.5	28.6	30.5	272	40.5	37	28.9	235	22.7	132	17.6	51	25.9	81
16	33.5	42.8	30.3	39.8	289	50.8	65	36.6	224	18.0	133	17.4	69	18.8	44
17	47.0	51.7	43.7	48.0	271	51.0	98	46.2	173	26.6	139	28.4	95	22.7	44
18	49.2	52.7	46.3	52.6	215	57.0	93	49.2	122	22.3	139	23.1	104	20.0	35
19	48.6	46.7	51.1	56.5	147	59.7	72	53.3	75	29.1	103	29.1	86	29.4	17
1971															
15-19	37.6	41.6	36.1	40.2	2,624	50.2	562	37.5	2,062	16.0	1,333	16.3	681	15.8	652
15	28.0	32.8	28.0	29.5	640	41.4	70	28.1	570	16.1	341	14.4	104	16.9	237
16	34.0	35.3	33.7	36.7	659	41.4	111	35.8	548	15.4	319	15.6	147	15.1	172
17	38.7	41.6	37.6	42.7	644	51.8	141	40.2	503	16.3	295	16.8	173	15.6	122
18	44.5	46.7	43.2	48.9	395	56.2	128	45.3	267	15.0	227	16.9	142	11.8	85
19	48.5	45.8	50.8	54.6	286	55.4	112	54.0	174	18.5	151	17.4	115	22.2	36

Source: M. Zelnik & J. F. Kantner, "Sexual and Contraceptive Experience of Young Unmarried Women in the United States, 1976 and 1971," Family Planning Perspectives, 9 (a) (March/April), 1977. Reprinted by permission.

TABLE 2.10

Table 2.10 presents the percent of never-married women aged 15 to 19 who correctly perceived the time of greatest risk of pregnancy within the menstrual cycle by age, race and sexual experience for 1971 and 1976. Data are from the National Survey of Young Women (NSYW).

Overall, a slightly higher proportion of never-married women aged 15 to 19 correctly perceived the time of greatest pregnancy risk within the menstrual cycle in 1976 compared to 1971, 40.6 compared to 37.6. In both years, sexually experienced young women were more likely than women not sexually experienced to perceive the time of greatest pregnancy risk within the menstrual cycle. Among whites, younger teenagers were less likely than older teenagers to be aware of the time of greatest risk. White women at all ages were more likely than black women to perceive the time of greatest pregnancy risk.

TABLE 2.11 Standardized Contraceptive-Use Failure Rates By User Characteristics And Method Type: Single Women, January 1, 1979 - July 1, 1982 (NSFG)

Characteristic	Method Type							
	Pill	IUD	Rhythm	Condom	Diaphragm	Spermacides	Other	No Method
Intent and Age[1]								
Delay								
Less than 18	4.5	4.4	15.9	7.8	14.2	15.5	9.1	33.5
18-19	3.1	4.9	17.5	8.7	15.7	17.1	10.1	36.5
20-24	4.5	4.3	15.7	7.7	14.0	15.2	9.0	33.0
25-29	3.4	3.2	12.0	5.8	10.7	11.7	6.8	26.0
30-44	3.9	3.8	13.9	6.8	12.4	13.5	7.9	29.8
Prevent								
Less than 18	11.0	10.5	33.9	18.4	31.6	34.0	21.1	62.9
18-19	9.6	9.3	30.6	16.3	28.3	30.5	18.7	58.2
20-24	7.2	6.9	23.9	12.3	21.7	23.5	14.2	47.6
25-29	5.0	4.8	17.4	8.6	15.6	17.0	10.0	36.3
30-44	1.9	1.8	7.0	3.3	6.2	6.8	3.9	15.7
Race[2]								
Black	4.5	4.3	2.3	7.7	13.9	15.1	8.9	32.5
Other Races	4.7	4.5	20.6	8.1	14.5	15.8	9.3	33.7
Parity[4]								
0 Live Births	3.9	3.8	14.1	6.8	12.3	13.4	7.9	29.5
1 + Live Births	6.6	6.3	22.4	11.2	20.0	21.6	13.0	44.3
Poverty Ratio Income[3]								
Less than 100%	5.4	5.2	18.6	9.3	16.7	18.2	10.8	38.2
100-299%	4.7	4.5	16.2	8.0	14.5	15.7	9.3	33.8
300% or more	3.9	3.7	13.7	6.7	12.2	13.2	7.8	29.0

[1] Standardized by race, parity, and poverty ratio income.
[2] Standardized by age, contraceptive intention, poverty ratio income and parity.
[3] Standardized by age, contraceptive intention, race and parity.
[4] Standardized by age, contraceptive intention, race and poverty ratio income.

Source: W.R. Grady, M.D. Hayward, J. Yagi, "Unintended Pregnancy in the United States: The Impact of Contraceptive Method and User Characteristics," *Family Planning Perspectives* (18) Sept./Oct.:200-209. Reprinted by permission.

TABLE 2.11

Table 2.11 presents standardized contraceptive-use failure rates by user characteristics and method type for characteristics and method type for single women. These data are for the period of January 1, 1979 to July 1, 1982 and are from the 1982 National Survey of Family Growth. Failure rates are the number of pregnancies occuring per 1,000 women using a given contraceptive method.

These data indicate substantial differences in contraceptive-use failure rates by user characteristics. Women under age 30 seeking to delay a pregnancy have lower use-failure rates than those seeking to prevent a pregnancy. Black women have higher use failure rates than women of other races. Women who had more than 3 live births had higher use failure rates than women who had fewer births. Women who had less than 100 percent of a poverty level income had higher contraceptive-use failure rates than women with higher income. Finally, women under age 18 seeking to prevent a pregnancy had the highest contraceptive-use failure rates regardless of other characteristics of the women.

III. PREGNANCY AMONG ADOLESCENTS

This section presents information on premarital and marital pregnancy, and pregnancy resolution among adolescents. The number of adolescent pregnancies is estimated by combining data on births available from the National Vital Statistics with data on abortions available from the Center for Disease Control and the Alan Guttmacher Institute and with an estimated proportion of miscarriages. These data are presented in Table 3.1.

Data on the number of pregnancies among sexually active women who do and do not use contraceptives by race, pregnancy intention, and other social characteristics are derived mainly from the National Longitudinal Survey of Youth (NLS), the National Surveys of Young Women and Men (NSYW/M), and the National Survey of Family Growth (NSFG). Because all three of these surveys are known to underestimate the proportion of adolescent women having abortions, they also underestimate the proportions of adolescent pregnancies.

TABLE 3.1 Reproductive Behavior: U.S. Women Aged 15-19, 1960-1984

	1970	1971	1972	1973	1974	1975	1976
Total Births	3,731,000	3,556,000	3,258,000	3,137,000	3,160,000	3,144,000	3,168,000
Births 15-19	644,708	627,942	616,280	604,096	595,449	582,238	558,744
Abortions	59,985*	150,598*	181,908*	232,440	279,790	326,780	362,680
Miscarriages	134,940	140,648	141,447	144,063	147,069	149,126	148,017
Pregnancies	839,633	919,188	939,635	980,599	1,022,308	1,058,144	1,069,441
Total Women 15-19	9,517,000	9,741,000	9,988,000	10,194,000	10,351,000	10,468,000	10,585,000
% Never Married	0.888	0.891	0.908	0.896	0.896	0.907	0.908
Total Never Married	8,451,096	8,679,231	9,069,104	9,133,824	9,274,496	9,494,476	9,611,180
% Single Sexually Experienced	0.250	0.270	0.280	0.300	0.320	0.340	0.350
Total Single Sexually Experienced	2,112,774	2,343,392	2,539,349	2,740,147	2,967,839	3,228,122	3,363,913
Total Ever Married	1,065,904	1,061,769	918,896	1,060,176	1,076,504	973,524	973,820
Total Sexually Experienced	3,178,678	3,405,161	3,458,245	3,800,323	4,044,343	4,201,646	4,337,733
Pregnancy Rate	0.088	0.094	0.094	0.096	0.099	0.101	0.101
Pregnancy Rate Sexually Experienced	0.264	0.270	0.272	0.258	0.253	0.252	0.247
Birth Rate	0.068	0.064	0.062	0.059	0.058	0.056	0.053
Birth Rate Sexually Experienced	0.203	0.184	0.178	0.159	0.147	0.139	0.129
Abortion Rate	0.006	0.015	0.018	0.023	0.027	0.031	0.034
Abortion Rate Sexually Experienced	0.019	0.044	0.053	0.061	0.069	0.078	0.084
Abortions/Pregnancies	0.071	0.164	0.194	0.237	0.274	0.309	0.339
Abortions/Abortions + Births	0.085	0.193	0.228	0.278	0.320	0.359	0.394
Abortions/Births	0.093	0.240	0.295	0.385	0.470	0.561	0.649

	1977	1978	1979	1980	1981	1982	1983	1984
Total Births	3,327,000	3,333,000	3,494,000	3,612,258	3,629,238	3,680,537	3,638,933	3,669,141
Births 15-19	555,154	543,407	549,472	552,161	527,392	513,758	489,286	469,682
Abortions	396,630	418,790	444,600	444,780	433,330	418,740	395,660	401,128**
Miscarriages	151,494	150,560	154,354	154,910	148,811	144,626	137,423	134,049
Pregnancies	1,107,278	1,112,757	1,148,426	1,151,851	1,109,533	1,077,124	1,022,369	1,004,859
Total Women 15-19	10,585,000	10,558,000	10,502,000	10,381,000	10,081,000	9,772,000	9,460,000	9,219,000
% Never Married	0.913	0.919	0.918	0.911	0.920	0.920	0.934	0.934
Total Never Married	9,664,105	9,702,802	9,640,836	9,457,091	9,274,520	8,990,240	8,835,640	8,610,546
% Single Sexually Experienced	0.360	0.380	0.390	0.400	0.420	0.430	0.430	0.430
Total Single Sexually Experienced	3,479,078	3,687,065	3,759,926	3,782,836	3,895,298	3,865,803	3,799,325	3,702,535
Total Ever Married	920,895	855,198	861,164	923,909	806,480	781,760	624,360	608,454
Total Sexually Experienced	4,399,973	4,542,263	4,621,090	4,706,745	4,701,778	4,647,563	4,423,685	4,310,989
Pregnancy Rate	0.105	0.105	0.109	0.111	0.110	0.110	0.108	0.109
Pregnancy Rate Sexually Experienced	0.252	0.245	0.249	0.245	0.236	0.232	0.231	0.233
Birth Rate	0.053	0.053	0.051	0.053	0.052	0.053	0.052	0.051
Birth Rate Sexually Experienced	0.127	0.120	0.119	0.117	0.112	0.111	0.111	0.109
Abortion Rate	0.037	0.040	0.042	0.043	0.043	0.043	0.042	0.044
Abortion Rate Sexually Experienced	0.090	0.092	0.096	0.094	0.092	0.090	0.089	0.093
Abortions/Pregnancies	0.358	0.376	0.387	0.386	0.391	0.389	0.387	0.399
Abortions/Abortions+Births	0.415	0.435	0.447	0.446	0.451	0.449	0.447	0.461
Abortions/Births	0.709	0.771	0.809	0.806	0.822	0.815	0.809	0.854

*Estimated number of legal abortions, which is recognized to underestimate the total number of abortions performed in that year.
**This estimate is based on the percentage of abortions to teenagers in 1982, which was 26.6 percent of all abortions.

TABLE 3.1 (continued)

Sources:

Births: 1960: U.S. Dept. HEW, NCHS, Vital Statistics of the United States, 1960, Vol I - Natility. USGPO:1962.
1965: U.S. Dept. HEW, NCHS, Vital Statistics of the United States, 1965, Vol I - Natility. USGPO:1967.
1970: U.S. Dept. HEW, NCHS, Vital Statistics of the United States, 1970, Vol I - Natility. USGPO:1965.
1971-1983: National Center of Health Statistics, Advance report of Final Natality Statistics, 1971-1983.

Abortions: 1960-1973: C. Tietze, "Repeat Abortions - Why More?" Family Planning Perspectives 10(Sept/Oct):286-288, 1978. Abortions to teens in 1960 and 1965 obtained by multiplying the estimated number of legal abortions to all women (from Tietze, 1978, above) by the estimated proportion obtained by teenagers (.33). Abortions to teens in 1970-1972 obtained by multiplying the estimated number of legal abortions to all women (from Tietze, 1978, above) by the estimated proportion obtained by teenagers in 1973 (.312).

1973-1980: from S. Henshaw (Ed.), "Abortion Services in the U.S., Each State and Metropolitan Area, 1979-80." Detailed Tables - Table 1. N.Y.: Alan Guttmacher Institute, 1983.

1980-81: from S. Henshaw, N. Binkin, E. Blaine, and J. Smith, "A Portrait of American Women Who Obtain Abortions," Family Planning Perspectives 17(March/April):90-96, 1985.

1982-1984: from S. Henshaw, "Trends in Abortions, 1982-1984," Family Planning Perspectives 18(Jan/Feb):34, 1986. Abortions for teens 15-19 in 1982-1984 obtained by multiplying the total number of legal abortions to women of all ages by the proportion of abortions to teens in 1981 (.275), the most recent year in which that distribution is available.

Number of teenagers and proportion single: See attached Table A

Proportion of teens sexually active: See Hofferth and Kohn, 1986.

Miscarriages: Miscarriages are calculated as 20% of births plus 10% of abortions, according to a model developed by C. Tietze and J. Bongaarts of the Population Council.

TABLE 3.1

Table 3.1 is a summary table of reproductive behavior of U.S. women aged 15 to 19 from 1960 to 1984. The sources of these data are outlined in detail at the end of the table. These are the most reliable national statistics available on pregnancies, births, abortions and miscarriages for adolescent women.

The pregnancy rate for women aged 15 to 19 declined between 1960 and 1965 but then rose steadily from 87 pregnancies per 1,000 women to 112 per 1,000 women in 1982. Recent data indicate a decline in the pregnancy rate to 109 per 1,000 women in 1984. The pregnancy rate calculated just for sexually experienced women, however, declined through the 1960s, 1970s and early 1980s from an estimated 458 pregnancies per 1,000 sexually active women to 233 pregnancies per 1,000 sexually active women. One result of this trend was a decrease in the number of births per 1,000 women aged 15 to 19 through the 1960s from 88 births per 1,000 women in 1960 to 51 births per 1,000 women in 1984. However, the decline in the birth rates for women aged 15 to 19 is also due to the increase in the abortion rate. The abortion rate for women aged 15 to 19 increased from an estimated 44 per 1,000 sexually active 15-to-19 year old women in 1960 to 93 per 1,000 sexually active women aged 15 to 19 in 1984.

TABLE 3.2 Pregnancies, Abortions, Miscarriages And Live Births By Marital Status To Women Aged 15 To 19, 1982

Category	Number	Percent
Total pregnancies to teens 15-19	1,077,124	100.0
Abortions	418,740	39.6
Miscarriages	144,626	13.4
Live births	513,758	47.0
Conceived post-maritally	145,907	13.4
Conceived premaritally, born post-maritally	118,678	10.9
Born premaritally	249,173	22.8

Source: See Table 4.1 for Source of Pregnancy, Abortion, Miscarriage and Live Birth Figures; O'Connell and Rogers 1984, derived from the 1982 Current Population Survey.

TABLE 3.2

Table 3.2 presents estimates of the total number of pregnancies, abortions, miscarriages, and live births by marital status to women aged 15 to 19 in 1982.

Of more than a million pregnancies to women aged 15 to 19 in 1982, less than half, 47 percent, are estimated to have resulted in live births; 39.6 percent ended in abortion; and about 13.4 percent were miscarriages. Thus, for every 10 adolescent pregnancies there were approximately 4 abortions, 1 miscarriage, and 5 births.

Of all pregnancies resulting in live births to women aged 15 to 19, 13.4 percent were conceived post-maritally, 10.9 percent were conceived premaritally and born post-maritally, and 22.8 percent were born premaritally.

TABLE 3.3 Proportion Of Women Ever-Pregnant Before Age 18 and Age 20, 1976 And 1981

	Percentage Experiencing a First Pregnancy by Age	
Year and Race	18	20
1976		
Total	23.7	41.1
1981		
Total	23.9	43.5
White	20.5	39.7
Black	40.7	63.1

Source: Calculated by Jacqueline Darroch Forrest, 1986; see Table 3.1 for source of data.

TABLE 3.3

Table 3.3 presents the proportion of all women ever experiencing a first pregnancy by age 18 and by age 20. In 1976, 23.7 percent of all women had a first pregnancy by age 18, 41.1 percent by age 20. In 1981, the proportions were slightly higher, 23.9 percent of the women experienced a first pregnancy by age 18, 43.5 percent by age 20. In 1981 a higher proportion of black women than white women had a first pregnancy by age 18, 40.7 compared to 20.5 percent and by age 20, 63.1 percent compared to 39.7 percent, respectively.

TABLE 3.4 Percentage of Premaritally Sexually Active Women Aged 15-19 Who Ever Experienced A Premarital First Pregnancy, By Contraceptive-Use Status* And Race, 1979 And 1976, Metropolitan U.S.

Contraceptive-Use Status	1979			1976		
	Total	White	Black	Total	White	Black
Always Used						
%	13.5	13.7	12.4	9.9	10.0	9.5
(N)	(307)	(165)	(142)	(203)	(98)	(105)
Used at 1st Intercourse, but not Always						
%	31.0	26.2	59.5	39.7	34.3	57.6
(N)	(119)	(73)	(46)	(66)	(36)	(30)
Did not use at 1st Intercourse, but at Some Time						
%	29.2	25.0	45.2	21.7	22.2	19.7
(N)	(241)	(137)	(104)	(171)	(95)	(76)
Never used						
%	62.2	58.8	70.3	49.5	41.5	65.2
(N)	(270)	(103)	(167)	(283)	(120)	(163)

*From first intercourse to first pregnancy or marriage, an interview.

Source: M. Zelnik and J. F. Kantner, 1980, "Sexual Activity, Contraceptive Use, and Pregnancy Among Metropolitan-Area Teenagers: 1971-1979," Family Planning Perspectives 12(5), (September/October), 1980. Reprinted by permission.

TABLE 3.4

Table 3.4 presents the percentage of premaritally sexually active women aged 15 to 19 who reported that they experienced a nonmarital first pregnancy, by contraceptive use status and race for 1979. The data are from the National Survey of Young Women (NSYW) for metropolitan areas only. As noted earlier, underreporting is a concern in surveys addressing sensitive topics such as nonmarital pregnancy.

Among sexually active women aged 15 to 19 who reported that they always used some form of contraception, 13.5 percent ever had a premarital pregnancy in 1979. Of women who said they used a contraceptive method at first intercourse but not consistently, 31 percent had a premarital pregnancy. Women who were premaritally sexually active and had never used contraception were the most likely to have ever experienced a premarital pregnancy, 62.2 percent in 1979.

White women aged 15 to 19 were less likely than black women to have ever experienced a premarital pregnancy, except among those who always used contraception, where whites were slightly more likely than blacks to have ever had a premarital pregnancy.

TABLE 3.5 Estimated Cumulative Percent Of Metropolitan-Area Females Aged 15-19 With Premarital First Pregnancy, By Duration Since First Intercourse, Race And Contraceptive Use Status, U.S., 1979

Months After First Intercourse	All Premaritally Sexually Experienced Females			Teens Who Never Used Contraceptive Methods			Teens Who Always Used Contraceptive Methods		
	Total	White	Black	Total	White	Black	Total	White	Black
3	13%	14%	14%	20%	21%	18%	4%	5%	2%
6	16	15	20	25	22	28	5	6	4
12	24	22	29	35	32	38	9	10	7
18	31	29	36	44	43	46	10	10	9
24	36	33	43	50	48	52	12	11	14

Source: M. Koenig and M. Zelnik, "The Risk of Premarital First Pregnancy Among Metropolitan-Area Teenagers: 1976 and 1979," Family Planning Perspectives 14(5):239-247, 1982. Reprinted by permission.

TABLE 3.5

The estimated cumulative percent of metropolitan-area females aged 15 to 19 with a premarital first pregnancy by duration since first intercourse, race and contraceptive use status in 1979 is presented in Table 3.5.

Within 24 months after first intercourse, 36 percent, or more than 1 out of every 3 premaritally sexually active teenagers, became pregnant. The difference between those who always used some method of contraception and those who had never used contraception was substantial. Within the first 3 months after intercourse, 20 percent of the teenagers who never used contraception became pregnant compared to only 4 percent of those who had always used contraception. By 24 months after first intercourse, half of the teenagers who had never used contraception had become pregnant while 12 percent of the teenagers who reported that they had always used a contraceptive method had become pregnant.

TABLE 3.6 Percentage Distributions Of Women Aged 15-19 Who Ever Experienced A Premarital First Pregnancy And Were Unmarried At The Time The Pregnancy Was Resolved, By Pregnancy Intention And, Among Those Who Did Not Want The Pregnancy, By Contraceptive Use, According To Race, 1979, 1976 And 1971* (Metropolitan-Area Teenagers)

Pregnancy Intention and Contraceptive Use	1979			1976			1971		
	Total	White	Black	Total	White	Black	Total	White	Black
Pregnancy Intention	(N=312)	(N=115)	(N=197)	(N=200)	(N=59)	(N=141)	(N=249)	(N=42)	(N=207)
Wanted	18.0	16.4	20.9	24.6	21.9	28.0	24.2	23.6	24.6
Not wanted	82.0	83.6	79.1	75.4	78.1	72.0	75.8	76.4	75.4
Did not want Pregnancy	(N=246)	(N=94)	(N=152)	(N=147)	(N=46)	(N=101)	(N=183)	(N=32)	(N=151)
Used Contraception	31.5	36.1	22.0	20.6	27.1	11.5	8.6	9.2	8.3
Did not use	68.5	63.9	78.0	79.4	72.9	88.5	91.4	90.6	91.7
Total	100.0	100.0	100.0	100.0	100.0	100.0	100.0	100.0	100.0

*Includes respondents pregnant at time of interview.

Source: M. Zelnik and J. F. Kantner. "Sexual Activity, Contraceptive Use and Pregnancy Among Metropolitan-Area Teenagers: 1971-1979." Family Planning Perspectives 12(5) (September/October), Table 6, 1980. Reprinted by permission.

TABLE 3.6

Table 3.6 shows the distribution of women aged 15 to 19 by race, in 1979, 1976, and 1971 who ever experienced a nonmarital pregnancy and were unmarried when the pregnancy was resolved, by pregnancy intention, and, among those who did not intend the pregnancy, by contraceptive use at the time of conception. Data are from the National Surveys of Young Women (NSYW) for metropolitan areas only. Again it is important to remember that under-reporting of pregnancies occurs in all surveys, and this could affect conclusions drawn from the data.

The data indicate that the percent of premarital pregnancies that were not intended in 1979 was slightly higher than in 1971--82 percent in 1979 compared to 76 percent in 1971. Black teenagers were slightly less likely than whites to describe their pregnancy as unwanted in 1971, 1976, and 1979.

Among teenagers who had an unintended premarital pregnancy the percent were using contraceptives were more than three times higher in 1979 than in 1971, 32 compared to 9 percent. Even so, black females who had an unintended premarital pregnancy were less likely to have used contraception than white females, especially in 1976 and 1979. Moreover, the great majority of unwanted premarital pregnancies in all years and in both race groups occurred to teens who were not using contraception.

IV. INDUCED ABORTION AMONG ADOLESCENTS

This section presents information on induced abortions among adolescent women in the United States. Data on abortions in the U.S. come from both federal and nonfederal sources. The Centers for Disease Control (CDC) carry out abortion surveillance which includes reports of abortions from most State health agencies, some hospitals, or from State participants in the Cooperative Health Statistics Registry of the National Center for Health Statistics (NCHS). Through this system, tabulations of abortions by characteristics are provided to CDC and released as an annual surveillance report. This report provides information on the distribution of abortions by age, race, parity and other characteristics.

The Alan Guttmacher Institute (AGI) contacts abortion service providers and thereby derives a more complete count of abortions, although no data are gathered regarding specific characteristics of the women. By combining information from both sources one can estimate the characteristics of women receiving abortions. For example, the CDC report of the percentage of abortions to teenagers can be applied to the total number of abortions reported through AGI. This is regularly done by AGI and CDC with some adjustments for differences in reporting systems, but it is not known how the characteristics of women differ in the two types of reporting.

NCHS obtains some individual level data through reports of induced abortions submitted to state vital registration offices. These data provide cross-classification of abortions by several characteristics, such as age, race and parity, but are obtained for a very limited number of states. For example, the report based on 1980 data covered only 295,932 abortions occurring in a twelve state area.

TABLE 4.1 Number And Percentage Distribution Of Legal Abortions, Abortion Rate Per 1,000 Women, And Percentage Of Pregnancies Terminated By Abortion, By Age Of Women, United States, Selected Years, 1974-1982

Measure	1973	1974	1977	1978	1979	1980	1981	1982
No. of Abortions	744,610	898,570	1,316,700	1,409,600	1,497,670	1,553,890	1,577,340	1,573,920
Less than 15	11,630	13,420	15,650	15,110	16,220	15,340	15,240	14,590
15-19	232,440	278,280	396,630	418,790	444,600	444,780	433,330	418,590
15-17	n.a.	u	(165,610)	(169,270)	(178,570)	(183,350)	(175,930)	(168,410)
18-19	n.a.	u	(231,020)	(249,520)	(266,030)	(261,430)	(257,400)	(250,330)
20-24	240,610	286,600	449,660	489,410	525,710	549,410	554,940	551,680
25-29	129,600	162,690	246,680	265,990	284,200	303,820	316,260	326,380
30-34	72,550	89,810	124,380	134,280	141,970	153,060	167,240	168,020
35-39	40,960	48,770	61,700	65,350	65,070	66,580	69,510	73,250
Greater than 40	16,820	19,000	22,000	20,670	19,900	20,900	20,820	21,260
% Distribution of Abortions								
Less than 15	1.6	1.5	1.2	1.1	1.1	1.0	1.0	0.9
15-19	31.2	31.0	30.1	29.7	29.7	28.6	27.5	26.6
15-17	n.a.	u	(12.6)	(12.0)	(11.9)	(11.8)	(11.2)	(10.7)
18-19	n.a.	u	(17.5)	(17.7)	(17.8)	(16.8)	(16.3)	(15.9)
20-24	32.3	31.9	34.2	34.7	35.1	35.4	35.2	35.0
25-29	17.4	18.1	18.7	18.9	19.0	19.6	20.0	20.7
30-34	9.7	10.0	9.4	9.5	9.5	9.8	10.6	10.7
35-39	5.5	5.4	4.7	4.6	4.3	4.3	4.4	4.7
Greater than 40	2.3	2.1	1.7	1.5	1.3	1.3	1.3	1.4
Total	100.0	100.0	100.0	100.0	100.0	100.0	100.0	100.0

Abortion Rate*	16.3	19.3	26.4	27.7	28.8	29.3	28.8
Less than 15+	5.6	6.4	7.6	7.5	8.3	8.4	8.3
15-19	22.8	26.9	37.5	39.7	42.4	42.9	42.9
15-17	n.a.	u	(26.2)	(26.9)	(28.8)	(30.2)	(30.1)
18-19	n.a.	u	(54.1)	(58.4)	(61.9)	(61.0)	(60.0)
20-24	26.2	30.4	44.3	47.2	49.9	51.4	51.2
25-29	16.4	19.6	26.9	28.4	29.6	30.8	31.5
30-34	10.9	13.0	15.7	16.4	16.5	17.1	17.7
35-39	7.1	8.4	9.8	9.8	9.4	9.3	9.3
Greater than 40***	2.9	3.3	3.9	3.6	3.4	3.5	3.3
% of Pregnancies Terminated by Abortions++	n.a.	22.0	28.6	29.2	29.6	30.0**	30.0
Less than 15	n.a.	29.0	41.1	40.9	43.0	42.7	43.3
15-19	n.a.		38.3	39.3	40.6	41.1	40.6
15-17	n.a.	u	(38.7)	(39.7)	(41.3)	42.4	41.7
18-19	n.a.	u	(37.9)	(39.3)	(40.1)	40.1	39.9
20-24	n.a.	20.0	27.6	28.7	29.4	30.1	30.2
25-29	n.a.	15.4	20.2	20.8	21.1	21.8	22.1
30-34	n.a.	21.7	23.7	23.5	23.0	23.3	24.2
35-39	n.a.	32.8	38.5	38.6	37.3	37.2	37.5
Greater than 40	n.a.	44.4	52.5	51.6	50.4	51.7	51.1

n.a.
n.a.
n.a.
n.a.
n.a.
n.a.
n.a.
n.a.
n.a.
n.a.
n.a.
n.a.
n.a.
n.a.
n.a.
n.a.
n.a.
n.a.
n.a.

TABLE 4.1 (continued)

*Denominator for total abortion rate is women aged 15-44.
**Based or estimated age distribution of women giving birth in 1981.
***Numerator is abortions obtained by women 40 and over; denominator is women aged 40-44.

+Numerator is abortions obtained by girls younger than 15; denominator is number of 14-year-old females.
++Denominator is live births six months later (to match time of conception with abortions). Pregnancies exclude miscarriages and stillbirths. Births and abortions are adjusted to age of woman at time of conception.

n.a. - not available.

Sources: S.K. Henshaw et al., Family Planning Perspectives Volume 15, No. 1, January/February 1983; S.K. Henshaw, et al, Family Planning Perspectives, Volume 17, No. 2, March/April 1985; Family Planning Perspectives, Volume 16, No. 3 May/June, 1984; Christopher Tietze and Stanley K. Henshaw, Induced Abortion: A World Review, 1986, New York, AGI, 1986; S.K. Henshaw "Trends in Abortions 1982-1984," Family Planning Perspectives, 18 (1) 1986.

TABLE 4.1

Table 4.1 presents the number and percentage distribution of legal abortions, the abortion rate and the percent of pregnancies terminated by abortion by the age of women. Data are tabulated by the Alan Guttmacher Institute (AGI) on the basis of its annual survey of clinics and other abortion providers combined with data on patient characteristics reported by most states to the Centers for Disease Control.

In 1982 there were 14,590 abortions to women under age 15, over 168,000 to women aged 15 to 17, and over 250,000 to women aged 18 to 19. Less than one percent of all abortions were obtained by women under age 15; 11 percent were to women aged 15 to 17; and 16 percent were to women aged 18 to 19. Nearly 30 percent of all abortions were to women less than 20 years of age.

The total abortion rate in 1982 was 28.8 abortions per 1,000 women aged 15 to 44. For young women less than 15 years of age the abortion rate was 8.6 per 1,000 women, only slightly higher than the 1974 rate. The abortion rate for women aged 15 to 19, however, increased from 27 to 43 per 1,000 women aged 15 to 19 between 1974 and 1982. The abortion rate (excluding miscarriages and stillbirths) for women aged 18 to 19 has consistently been about twice as high as the rate for women aged 15 to 17.

The proportion of pregnancies terminated by abortion for 15-to 19-year-old women increased by 40 percent from 1974 to 1981, from 29 to 40.6 percent. In 1981, 4 in 10 pregnancies among teens ended in induced abortion. The proportion of pregnancies to women younger than 20 terminated by abortion was higher than for any other age group with the exception of women over 40 years of age, (among whom 51 percent of pregnancies end in abortion).

The number of abortions, the rate, the ratio, and the percent of pregnancies ending in abortion rose rapidly between 1973 and 1979. In 1982, however, the abortion rate and ratio, and the number of abortions obtained by teenagers declined slightly.

TABLE 4.2 Percent Change In Abortion Rates And In The Number Of Pregnancies Terminated By Abortions By Age Group, 1974 To 1978, 1979 To 1981, 1981 To 1982

	% Change 1974-78		% Change 1979-81		% Change 1981-82	
Age Group	In Abortion Rate	In % Of Pregnancies Terminated By Abortions	In Abortion Rate	In % Of Pregnancies Terminated By Abortions	In Abortion Rate	In % Of Pregnancies Terminated By Abortions
Less than 15	+17	n.a.	+4	+0.7	-3	n.a.
15-19	+48	+36	+2	0	-1	n.a.
20-24	+55	+44	+2	+3	-0.2	n.a.
25-29	+45	+35	+6	+5	+0.3	n.a.
30-34	+26	+8	+7	+5	0	n.a.
35-39	+17	+18	+1	+0.5	-2	n.a.
Greater than 40	+9	+16	0	+1	-3	n.a.

n.a. - not available

Source: See Table 4.1

TABLE 4.2

The percent change in abortion rates and in the number of pregnancies terminated by abortion from 1974 to 1982 by age are shown in Table 4.2. As in Table 4.1, data are from the Alan Guttmacher Institute and the Centers for Disease Control (CDC).

The abortion rate increased between 1974 and 1978 by 17 percent among women younger than age 15, 48 percent among women aged 15 to 19 and 55 percent among women aged 20 to 24. The increase in the proportion of pregnancies terminated by abortion was 36 percent for women aged 15 to 19, and 44 percent for women aged 20 to 24.

The changes in the abortion rate and in the percent of pregnancies terminated by abortion were much lower between 1979 and 1981. The abortion rate increased by 4 percent for women under age 15 from 1979 to 1981, by 2 percent for women aged 15 to 19, and 2 percent for women aged 20 to 24. The proportion of pregnancies terminated by abortion rose less than one percent between 1979 and 1981 for young women under age 15, not at all for women aged 15 to 19, and 3 percent for women aged 20 to 24.

For all women under age 20, there were slight decreases in the abortion rates between 1981 and 1982. Data on the percent of pregnancies terminated by abortion for 1982 were not available.

TABLE 4.3 Abortion Rate* Per 1,000 Women, By Age-group And Race, According To Marital Status, 1979-81

Characteristics	Married	Unmarried
Age-Group and Race		
All Races**		
Less than 15***	--	8.4
15-19	17.7	31.3
15-17	15.4	21.7
18-19	18.4	47.0
20-24	14.1	50.3
25-29	9.4	41.6
30-34	6.0	25.7
35-39	2.7	9.0
White	6.5	33.3
Black	15.1	41.7

Note: Includes separated, divorced, widowed and never-married women

*Rates are three-year averages of induced terminations of pregnancy per 1,000 population of residence.
**Includes races other than Black and White.
***There is no accurate estimate of the number of married women under 15.

Sources: Abortions by aged-group and marital status--data on 11 states (Colorado, Kansas, Missouri, Montana, Oregon, Rhode Island, South Carolina, Tennessee, Utah, Vermont and Virginia). K. Prager, "Induced Terminations of Pregnancy: Reporting States, 1981" NCHS, <u>Monthly Vital Statistics Report</u>, Vol. 34, No. 4, July 1985.

TABLE 4.3

Table 4.3 shows the abortion rate per 1,000 women by age and marital status and by race and marital status for 1979-1981. Data are provided by 11 states to the National Center for Health Statistics (NCHS).

Abortion rates in general were higher among unmarried women than among married women. The highest abortion rates among unmarried women were between the ages of 18 and 29, while the highest abortion rates for married women were for those women under age 20.

Black women were considerably more likely to have an abortion than white women, particularly black married women. The abortion rates for black women for the 1979-1981 period were 15.1 per 1,000 married women and 41.7 per 1,000 unmarried women. For white women, the abortion rates were 6.5 per 1,000 married women and 33.3 per 1,000 unmarried women.

TABLE 4.4 Estimated Abortion Rate Per 1,000 Women Aged 12-19* By Race, United States, 1971-1978

Year	Abortion Rate		Ratio of Black Rate to White Rate
	White	Black and Other**	
1972	11.7	17.4	1.5
1973	14.1	25.4	1.8
1974	16.0	34.0	2.1
1975	18.0	42.0	2.3
1976	19.8	48.1	2.4
1977	22.2	50.7	2.3
1978	24.3	51.2	2.1

*Based on age at conception.
**Including teenagers of all other racial minorities.

Source: N.V. Ezzard, W. Cates, Jr., D.G. Kramer, and C. Tietze, "Race- Specific Patterns of Abortion Use by American Teenagers," American Journal of Public Health, 72: 809, 1982. Reprinted by permission.

TABLE 4.4

Table 4.4 shows the estimated abortion rate per 1,000 females aged 12 to 19 by race from 1972 to 1978. These data are from the Centers for Disease Control (CDC).

The rate of abortion per 1,000 women more than doubled between 1972 and 1978 for teenagers of both races. For every 1,000 white women there were 11 abortions in 1972 and 24 abortions in 1978. The abortion rate was 17 per one thousand black women in 1972 and 51 per 1,000 in 1978. By 1978 the abortion rate for black teenagers had increased to twice the rate for whites.

TABLE 4.5 Legal Abortions Per 1,000 Births (Abortion Ratio) By Age At Conception And By Race, United States, 1972-1978

Year	Age Less Than 15		Age 15-17		Age 18-19		Teenagers Age 12-19		Ratio of Black Ratio To White Ratio
	White	Black & Other	White	Black & Other	White	Black & Other	White	Black & Other	
1972	393	221	268	158	264	210	270	186	0.7
1973	419	301	332	245	339	322	338	283	0.8
1974	427	397	385	346	388	449	388	395	1.0
1975	489	505	456	457	441	551	449	503	1.1
1976	515	595	533	558	491	649	509	602	1.2
1977	568	612	603	597	526	660	558	627	1.1
1978	617	629	665	620	581	668	615	643	1.0

Source: See Table 4.4.

TABLE 4.5

Table 4.5 shows the number of legal abortions per 1,000 births (Abortion Ratio) by age at conception by race from 1972 to 1978. The data on abortions are from the Center for Disease Control (CDC) and the data on births are from National Center for Health Statistics (NCHS).

From 1972 to 1978, the ratio of abortions per 1,000 live births more than doubled for all women aged 12 to 19 at conception. There were 270 abortions for every 1,000 live births to white teenage women in 1972 and 615 per 1,000 in 1978. The ratio of abortions per 1,000 live births for nonwhite (black and other) teenage women was lower than for white in 1972. Between 1972 and 1978, the ratio rose more rapidly among nonwhite teenagers than among white teenagers, and in 1978 the nonwhite ratio exceeded the white ratio for teenagers under age 15 and ages 18 and 19.

TABLE 4.6 Ratios of Induced Terminations of Pregnancy By Race And Age Of Woman, 1980: 12-State Area (Ratios Per 1,000 Live Births. Induced Terminations of Pregnancy And Live Births Are Only Those Occurring In The Area Among Residents Of The Area)

	Ratio		
Age of Woman	All Races[a]	White	Black
All Ages	388.2	1,337.7	638.7
Under 14 years	1,868.1	2,085.2	1,749.6
14 years	1,380.6	1,632.0	1,200.2
15-19 years	738.7	786.3	644.5
15 years	975.4	1,177.1	774.9
16 years	894.0	1,042.8	673.4
17 years	765.4	841.8	621.2
18 years	794.1	847.5	669.0
19 years	603.1	613.0	591.5
20-24 years	411.6	362.2	638.6
25-29 years	247.7	197.1	580.1
30-34 years	254.2	201.7	598.3
35-39 years	443.2	371.0	836.5
40 years and over	837.8	784.5	1,120.3

Note: The 12-State area includes Colorado, Kansas, Missouri, Montana, New York, Oregon, Rhode Island, South Carolina, Tennessee, Utah, Vermont, and Virginia.

[a] Includes races other than white and black.

Source: Burnham, 1983: Table A; see references at end of this volume.

TABLE 4.6

Table 4.6 presents the number of induced terminations of pregnancy or abortions per 1,000 live births (abortion ratio) by race and age of women for the 12 state reporting area in 1980. The data, collected from 12 states, are provided by National Center for Health Statistics (NCHS).

For women of all ages and races, there were 388 abortions per 1,000 live births. The abortion ratio was highest among women under age 20. For women under age 14 there were 1,868 abortions per 1,000 live births, and for women aged 14 there were 1,380 abortions per 1,000 live births.

For all ages under age 20, the abortion ratio was higher for white women than for black women. Among women aged 20 and over, however, the number of abortions per 1,000 live births was higher for black women than for white women.

TABLE 4.7 Percent of Induced Terminations of Pregnancy To Women With No Previous Induced Termination, By Age And Race Of Women: 12-State Area, 1980 (Data Include Only Induced Terminations Of Pregnancy Occurring In The Reporting Area)

Age of Woman	Ratio		
	All[a] Races	White	Black
All Ages	65.7	68.9	57.8
Under 15 years	94.7	96.0	93.5
15-17 years	87.6	89.1	83.9
18-19 years	77.6	79.6	70.8
20-24 years	62.2	65.1	54.5
25-19 years	54.8	57.9	47.1
30-34 years	56.4	60.0	47.0
35-39 years	60.1	65.8	48.0
40 years and over	67.2	72.2	54.5

Note: The 12-State area includes Colorado, Kansas, Missouri, Montana, New York, Oregon, Rhode Island, South Carolina, Tennessee, Utah, Vermont, and Virginia.

[a] Includes races other than white and black.

Source: Burnham, 1983: Table E.; see references at the end of this volume.

TABLE 4.7

Table 4.7 shows the proportion of abortions obtained by women with no previous induced termination, by age and race of women for the 12 state reporting area in 1980. The data are from the National Center for Health Statistics (NCHS).

The large majority of women, regardless of race, under age 20 having an abortion in 1980 were having their first abortion. Among young women under age 15, 94.7 percent had not had a previous abortion--96.0 percent of white women and 93.5 percent of black women. Among women aged 15 to 17 having an abortion, 87.6 percent had not had previous abortion--89.1 percent of white women and 83.9 percent of black women. Finally, among women aged 18 to 19 having an abortion in 1980, 77.6 percent had not had a previous abortion--79.6 percent of white women and 70.8 percent of black women.

V. MARRIAGE AMONG PREGNANT ADOLESCENTS

This section presents information on marriage among pregnant adolescents and adolescents who have a first birth in the United States. The focus is on the marital status of the adolescent female at conception, at birth and after birth.

The data presented in the following tables are from the Current Population Surveys (CPS), the 1982 National Survey of Family Growth and the National Surveys of Young Women and Men (NSYW/M). They show that consistent with the decline in marriage among all teenagers, there has been an increase in the proportion of teenage women who remain unmarried after the birth of their child. These data permit comparisons by race but not by ethnic group.

TABLE 5.1 Percent Of Males And Females Aged 15 to 19 Never-Married, By Race And Ethnicity[1], 1960-1985

Year	Category	Males			Females		
		15-17	18-19	15-19	15-17	18-19	15-19
1960	Total	99.1	91.1	96.3	93.2	67.8	83.9
	White	99.1	91.0	96.2	93.3	67.6	83.9
	Nonwhite	99.2	91.9	96.6	92.3	69.3	83.8
1970	Total	98.6	91.3	95.9	95.3	76.6	88.1
	White	98.7	91.3	95.9	95.4	76.4	88.0
	Black	98.0	91.0	95.5	95.0	77.7	88.6
	Hispanic	97.7	87.4	94.0	93.1	70.6	84.7
1973	Total	99.2*	90.4	96.5*	96.2	75.8	89.6*
	White	99.1*	89.5	96.2*	96.2	74.4	89.1*
	Non-white	99.5*	95.6	98.4*	96.1	83.9	92.2*
	Hispanic	n.a.	n.a.	n.a.	n.a.	n.a.	n.a.
1976	Total	99.4*	91.9	97.0*	97.0*	78.3	90.8*
	White	99.3*	91.2	96.7*	96.8*	77.2	90.2*
	Black	99.6*	95.9	98.5*	98.1*	85.0	93.8*
	Hispanic	99.5*	92.7	97.7*	94.6*	74.9	87.1*
1980	Total	99.4	94.2	97.3	97.0	82.8	91.1
	White	99.4	93.6	97.0	96.7	81.5	90.4
	Black	99.4	97.7	98.8	98.3	90.9	95.4
	Hispanic	98.5	92.2	95.8	94.6	79.2	88.2
1981	Total	99.2	95.7	97.8	97.2	84.7	92.0
	White	99.2	95.4	97.7	96.9	83.4	91.3
	Black	99.6	97.0	98.6	98.8	92.7	96.4
	Hispanic	99.2	91.8	96.3	95.3	74.0	86.7
1984	Total	99.7	96.8	98.5	98.0	87.1	93.4
	White	99.6	96.5	98.3	97.7	85.2	92.4
	Black	100.0	98.2	99.3	99.3	97.2	98.4
	Hispanic	99.0	93.5	96.8	95.7	79.1	88.8
1985	Total	99.7	97.1	98.7	98.0	86.7	93.4

[1]Hispanic persons may be of any race and Black and White totals may include Hispanics.

n.a. = not available

*Includes males and females 14 years of age.

Source: U.S. Bureau of the Census, "Marital Status and Living Arrangements", CPR, Series P-20, 1960, 1970, 1973, 1975, 1976, 1981, 1984, 1985; <u>Statistical Abstract of the U.S.: 1985</u>, Washington, D.C., 1986.

TABLE 5.1

Table 5.1 presents the proportion of males and females never-married by race from 1960 to 1985 (breakdowns by race were not available for 1985). There was a gradual increase in the proportion of men who remained single until at least age 20 and a rather striking delay in marriage among young women. The percent of unmarried females aged 15 to 19 rose by about 11 percent and the percent of unmarried males aged 15 to 19 rose about 2 percent between 1960 and 1985. Most of this increase was for 18 and 19 year old women. The proportion of females who were single rose by 28 percent for 18 and 19 year old women.

The increasing tendency to remain single was more dramatic for black females aged 18 and 19 than for white and Hispanic females aged 18 and 19. While the proportions of black and white 18 to 19 year-old females who were unmarried were similar in 1970, by 1984 the proportion unmarried was 12 percentage points higher among blacks. The proportion of Hispanic females 18 to 19 years old who were unmarried was consistently lower than for either whites or blacks, even though 8.5 percentage points higher in 1984 than 1970. The percent increase in the proportion of black females aged 18 to 19 was 25 percent compared to 12 percent for both white and Hispanic females.

TABLE 5.2 Percentage Of First-Born Babies Born to Mothers Aged 15-19, Conceived Either Maritally or Extra-Maritally, By Race, Age, and Marital Status at First Birth According To Birth Cohort Of Baby (numbers, in 1,000s, shown in parentheses)

	Birth Cohort of Baby						
	1950-1954	1955-1959	1960-1964	1965-1969	1970-1974	1975-1979	1980-1981
All Women Aged 15-19	(1,388)	(1,739)	(1,957)	(2,112)	(2,435)	(2,061)	(622)*
Conceived/born in wedlock	69.9	60.6	54.0	45.6	33.6	32.5	28.4
Conceived/born out-of-wedlock	16.1	18.3	22.4	24.2	35.2	44.5	48.5
Conceived out-of wedlock/born in wedlock	14.0	21.0	23.6	30.4	31.2	23.0	23.1
White Women Aged 15-19	(1,120)	(1,400)	(1,574)	(1,633)	(1,746)	(1,469)	(500)*
Conceived/born in wedlock	77.4	68.6	61.7	52.3	42.7	41.9	35.6
Conceived/born out-of-wedlock	9.4	10.6	13.7	14.5	20.2	30.3	36.8
Conceived out-of wedlock/born in wedlock	13.2	20.8	24.7	33.3	37.1	27.8	27.6
Black Women Aged 15-19	(251)	(316)	(343)	(429)	(641)	(542)	(141)*
Conceived/born in wedlock	35.1	24.7	18.9	18.9	8.9	6.6	3.5
Conceived/born out-of-wedlock	46.6	52.8	62.1	61.3	75.7	83.2	87.9
Conceived out-of wedlock/born in wedlock	18.3	22.5	19.0	19.8	15.4	10.1	8.5

*Data are incomplete for this cohort and may underestimate out of wedlock births.

Source: M. O'Connell and C.C. Rogers, Family Planning Perspectives, Volume 16, No. 4, July/August 1984; Data are derived from June 1980 and June 1982 CPS.

TABLE 5.2

The percentage of first babies born to mothers aged 15 to 19, by race and marital status at conception, and at first birth by the birth cohort of the baby, is presented in Table 5.2. Data are from the Current Population Surveys (CPS).

Overall, the percent of first-born babies conceived out of wedlock from 1980 to 1981 was more than twice the percent conceived out of wedlock from 1950 to 1954 (72 and 30 percent respectively). Of the babies conceived out of wedlock from 1950 to 54, about one-half were born out of wedlock. In contrast, seven out of every ten babies conceived out of wedlock and born between 1980 and 1981, were born out-of-wedlock. This represents a tripling in the proportion of babies born to single teenagers (16 percent between 1950 and 1954 compared to 49 percent between 1980 and 1981).

Black teenagers were much more likely to both conceive and give birth out-of-wedlock than white teenagers. Almost two-thirds (65 percent) of all first births to black women aged 15 to 19 from 1950 to 1954 and over 96 percent from 1980 to 1982 were babies conceived out of wedlock. Out of those conceived out of wedlock, seven out of every ten babies born between 1950 and 1954 and nine out of every ten babies born between 1980 and 1981 were born to single mothers. The increase in the percent of all first born babies conceived and born out of wedlock to black women was almost 90 percent from 1950-54 to 1980-81 (47 and 88 percent respectively).

In comparison, less than 25 percent of all first births to white women, between 1950 to 1954, but about two-thirds born from 1980 to 1981 were conceived out-of-wedlock. From 1950 to 1954 approximately 1 out of every 5 babies conceived out-of-wedlock was born out-of-wedlock; from 1980 to 1981, 3 out of every five premaritally pregnant white teens were still single at the birth of their first child. The proportion of all first born babies conceived and born out-of-wedlock to white women nearly quadrupled from 9 percent between 1950 and 1954 to 37 percent between 1980 and 1981.

VI. BIRTHS TO ADOLESCENTS

This section presents information on the number of births to U.S. adolescents by the mother's age, race, ethnicity, and marital status, and by the father's age and race. Data on first births occurring to adolescent females as well as birth rates are presented. Also included are data on prenatal care among adolescent mothers and infant mortality rates for babies born to adolescent mothers.

In the following tables, the data on births to adolescents are from the National Vital Statistics and the 1980 National Natality Survey. The data on births by mother's age and race are considered to be very reliable. However, the data on birth to fathers are less reliable because there is a substantial under-reporting of the age of the father by adolescent females. Despite these limitations data are presented in order to provide a rough indication of the age of fathers of babies born to adolescent mothers. Data on births to adolescent males and females from the National Longitudinal Survey (NLS) are also presented and the same caution on under-reporting of fatherhood by males is relevant.

Data on births to adolescent mothers of Hispanic origin are presented separately to show variations among mothers of Hispanic origin and because comparable time series of data are not available for Hispanic origin mothers.

TABLE 6.1 Number Of Births In The United States To Women Under Age Twenty By Race, 1955-1984

Year	All Races Under 15	All Races 15-17	All Races 18-19	Whites Under 15	Whites 15-17	Whites 18-19	Non-Whites Under 15	Non-Whites 15-17	Non-Whites 18-19	Blacks* Under 15	Blacks* 15-17	Blacks* 18-19
1984	9,965	166,726	302,938	3,959	105,016	215,937	6,006	61,728	87,001	5,720	56,907	77,485
1983	9,752	172,673	316,613	4,031	109,641	228,511	5,721	63,032	88,102	5,439	58,160	78,506
1982	9,773	181,162	332,596	4,153	115,869	242,079	5,620	65,293	90,517	5,395	60,282	80,252
1981	9,632	187,397	339,995	3,970	120,913	249,100	5,662	66,484	90,895	5,425	61,850	81,428
1980	10,169	198,222	353,939	4,171	127,657	260,401	5,998	70,565	93,538	5,793	65,966	84,387
1979	10,699	200,137	349,335	4,402	127,970	255,837	6,297	72,167	93,498	6,139	67,728	85,077
1978	10,772	202,661	340,746	4,512	130,957	249,103	6,260	71,704	91,643	6,068	71,182	83,684
1977	11,455	213,788	345,366	4,671	138,223	253,960	6,784	75,565	91,406	6,582	71,182	84,008
1976	11,928	215,493	343,251	5,054	139,901	253,374	6,874	75,592	89,877	6,661	71,429	82,507
1975	12,642	227,270	354,968	5,073	148,344	261,785	7,569	78,926	93,183	7,315	74,946	86,098
1974	12,529	234,177	361,272	5,053	152,257	267,895	7,476	81,920	93,377	7,291	77,947	86,483
1973	12,861	238,403	365,693	4,907	153,416	271,417	7,954	84,987	94,276	7,778	81,158	87,615
1972	12,082	236,641	379,639	4,573	150,897	283,089	7,509	85,744	96,550	7,363	82,217	90,132
1971	11,578	226,298	401,644	4,130	143,806	302,920	7,448	82,492	98,724	7,264	79,238	92,446
1970	11,752	223,590	421,118	4,320	143,646	319,962	7,432	79,944	101,156	7,274	76,882	94,944
1969	10,468	201,770	402,884	3,684	128,156	306,118	6,784	73,614	96,766	6,650	71,020	90,918
1968	9,504	192,970	398,342	3,114	121,166	305,336	6,390	71,804	93,006	6,312	69,594	87,986
1967	8,593	188,234	408,211	2,761	118,035	317,204	5,832	70,199	91,007	5,742	68,133	86,410
1966	8,128	186,704	434,722	2,666	119,800	345,312	5,462	66,904	89,410	5,370	64,922	84,818
1965	7,768	188,604	402,290	2,444	124,294	319,460	5,324	64,310	82,830			
1964	7,816	196,220	389,490	2,676	134,596	309,762	5,140	61,624	79,728			
1963	7,594	180,564	405,890	2,584	132,096	321,212	4,814	54,848	75,662			
1962	7,340	172,836	427,462	2,690	117,660	342,172	4,520	51,818	75,970			
1961	7,462	177,894	423,826	2,808	125,194	346,512	4,654	52,700	77,314			
1960	6,780	182,408	404,558	2,524	129,544	328,586	4,256	52,864	75,972			
1959	6,776	177,786	393,262	2,572	125,822	319,548	4,204	51,964	73,714			
1958	6,648	171,786	382,418	2,648	121,704	310,992	4,000	50,082	71,426			
1957	6,960	170,716	379,496	2,648	120,040	308,934	4,312	50,676	70,562			
1956	6,356	160,580	359,842	2,348	112,184	290,638	4,008	48,396	69,204			
1955	5,883	149,722	334,375	2,136	103,503	269,175	3,747	46,219	65,200			

*Data for Blacks separately are not available prior to 1969. Blacks included among non-Whites in all years.

Source: National Center for Health Statistics, Vital Statistics of the United States, annual volumes; NCHS, "Advanced Report of Final Natality Statistics" Monthly Vital Statistics Report, Vol. 34, No. 6, September 1985 and Vol. 35, No. 4, July 1986.

TABLE 6.1

Table 6.1 shows the number of births by age of mother for females under 20, by race from 1955 to 1984. In general, the number of births to females under age 20 gradually increased from 1955 through the early 1970s and then began to steadily decline primarily due to changes in the number of women in these age groups. See table 6.2 for data concerning the changes in births relative to the population of young women.

TABLE 6.2 Birth Rates By Age Of Mother, By Race Of Child, United States, 1950-1984 (births per 1,000 women, by age and race)

Year and Race of Child	Age of Mother									
	10-14 Years	15-19 Years			20-24 Years	25-29 Years	30-34 Years	35-39 Years	40-44 Years	45-49 Years
		Total	15-17	18-19						

Year	10-14	Total	15-17	18-19	20-24	25-29	30-34	35-39	40-44	45-49
All Races										
1984	1.2	50.9	31.1	78.3	107.3	108.3	66.5	22.8	3.9	0.2
1983	1.1	51.7	32.0	78.1	108.3	108.7	64.6	22.1	3.8	0.2
1982	1.1	52.9	32.4	80.7	111.3	111.0	64.2	21.1	3.9	0.2
1981	1.1	52.7	32.1	81.7	111.8	112.0	61.4	20.0	3.8	0.2
1980	1.1	53.0	32.5	82.1	115.1	112.9	61.9	19.8	3.9	0.2
1979	1.2	52.3	32.3	81.3	112.8	111.4	60.3	19.5	3.9	0.2
1978	1.2	51.5	32.2	79.8	109.9	108.5	57.8	19.0	3.9	0.2
1977	1.2	52.8	33.9	80.9	112.9	111.0	56.4	19.2	4.2	0.2
1976	1.2	52.8	34.1	80.5	110.3	106.2	53.6	19.0	4.3	0.2
1975	1.3	55.6	36.1	85.0	113.0	108.2	52.3	19.5	4.6	0.3
1974	1.2	57.5	37.3	88.7	117.7	111.5	53.8	20.2	4.8	0.3
1973	1.2	59.3	38.5	91.2	119.7	112.2	55.6	22.1	5.4	0.3
1972	1.2	61.7	39.0	96.9	130.2	117.7	59.8	24.8	6.2	0.4
1971	1.1	64.5	38.2	105.3	150.3	134.1	67.3	28.7	7.1	0.4
1970	1.2	68.3	38.8	114.7	167.8	145.1	73.3	31.7	8.1	0.5
1965	0.8	70.4	--	--	196.8	162.5	95.0	46.4	12.8	0.8
1960	0.8	89.1	--	--	258.1	197.4	112.7	56.2	15.5	0.9
1955	0.9	90.3	--	--	241.6	190.2	116.0	58.6	16.1	1.0
1950	1.0	81.6	--	--	196.6	166.1	103.7	52.9	15.1	1.2

White									
1984	0.6	42.5	23.9	68.1	101.4	107.7	66.1	21.7	3.5	0.2
1983	0.6	43.6	24.8	68.3	102.6	108.0	64.0	21.0	3.5	0.2
1982	0.6	44.6	25.2	70.8	105.9	110.3	63.3	20.0	3.5	0.2
1981	0.5	44.6	25.1	71.9	106.3	111.3	60.2	18.7	3.4	0.2
1980	0.6	44.7	25.2	72.1	109.5	112.4	60.4	18.5	3.4	0.2
1979	0.6	43.7	24.7	71.0	107.0	110.8	59.0	18.3	3.5	0.2
1978	0.6	42.9	24.9	69.4	104.1	107.9	56.6	17.7	3.5	0.2
1977	0.6	44.1	26.1	70.5	107.7	110.9	55.3	18.0	3.8	0.2
1976	0.6	44.1	26.3	70.2	105.3	105.9	52.6	17.8	3.9	0.2
1975	0.6	46.4	28.0	74.0	108.2	108.1	51.3	18.2	4.2	0.2
1974	0.6	47.9	28.7	77.3	113.0	111.8	52.9	18.9	4.4	0.2
1973	0.6	49.0	29.2	79.3	114.4	112.3	54.4	20.7	4.9	0.3
1972	0.5	51.0	29.3	84.3	124.8	117.4	58.4	23.3	5.6	0.3
1971	0.5	53.6	28.5	92.3	144.9	134.0	65.4	26.9	6.4	0.4
1970	0.5	57.4	29.2	101.5	163.4	145.9	71.9	30.0	7.5	0.4
1965	0.3	60.7	--	--	189.8	158.8	91.7	44.1	12.0	0.7
1960	0.4	79.4	--	--	252.8	194.9	109.6	54.0	14.7	0.8
1955	0.3	79.1	--	--	235.8	186.6	114.0	56.7	15.4	0.9
1950	0.4	70.0	--	--	190.4	165.1	102.6	51.4	14.5	1.0
Black									
1984	4.3	95.7	69.7	132.0	137.9	103.2	59.5	24.8	5.1	0.2
1983	4.1	95.5	70.1	130.4	137.7	103.4	59.2	24.7	5.2	0.3
1982	4.1	97.0	71.2	133.3	139.1	106.9	60.4	24.2	5.4	0.4
1981	4.1	97.1	70.6	135.9	141.2	108.3	60.4	24.2	5.6	0.3
1980	4.3	100.0	73.6	138.8	146.3	109.1	62.9	24.5	5.8	0.3
1979	4.6	101.7	75.7	140.4	146.3	108.2	60.7	24.7	6.1	0.4
1978	4.4	100.9	75.0	139.7	143.8	105.4	58.3	24.3	6.1	0.4
1977	4.7	104.7	79.6	142.9	144.4	106.4	57.5	25.4	6.6	0.5
1976	4.7	104.9	80.3	142.5	140.5	101.6	53.6	24.8	6.8	0.5
1975	5.1	111.8	85.6	152.4	142.8	102.2	53.1	25.6	7.5	0.5

TABLE 6.2 (continued)

Year and Race of Child	Age of Mother								
	10-14 Years	15-19 Years			20-24 Years	25-29 Years	30-34 Years	35-39 Years	40-44 Years	45-49 Years
		Total	15-17	18-19						
1974	5.0	116.5	90.0	158.7	146.7	102.2	54.1	27.0	7.6	0.6
1973	5.4	123.1	96.0	166.6	153.1	103.9	58.1	29.4	8.6	0.6
1972	5.1	129.8	99.5	179.5	165.0	112.4	64.0	33.4	9.8	0.7
1971	5.1	134.5	99.4	192.6	186.6	128.0	74.8	38.9	11.6	0.9
1970	5.2	147.7	101.4	204.9	202.7	136.3	79.6	41.9	12.5	1.0
1965	4.3	140.6	--	--	247.8	183.2	114.9	62.7	18.7	1.4
1960	4.3	156.1	--	--	295.4	218.6	137.1	73.9	21.9	1.1

Source: National Center for Health Statistics, Vital Statistics of the United States, annual volumes, see Table 6.1.

TABLE 6.2

Table 6.2 shows the birth rates by age of mother and race of child from 1950 to 1984. Data are from National Center for Health Statistics (NCHS) and U.S. Bureau of Census. In general, there was a decline in the rate of births per 1,000 women between 1950 and 1984 for women aged 15 to 49. The decline was most steep among older women. The birth rate for women aged 15 to 19 declined by 25 percent between 1970 to 1984, from 68.3 to 50.9 births per 1,000 women. Between 1970 and 1984 the birth rate for teenagers aged 15 to 17 declined by about 20 percent (from 38.8 to 31.1 per 1,000) compared to a decline of 32 percent for women aged 18 to 19 (from 114.7 to 78.3 per 1,000).

The birth rates for black teenage women have consistently been at least two times higher than the rates for white women even though there was a decline in the birth rates for both races. For white women in 1984 there were 42.5 births per 1,000 women aged 15 to 19, 24 births per 1,000 women aged 15 to 17 and 68 births per 1,000 women aged 18 to 19. These rates had decreased by 26, 18 and 33 percent respectively from 1970 to 1984. For black women there were about 96 births per 1,000 women aged 15 to 19, 70 per 1,000 for women aged 15 to 17 and 132 per 1,000 for women aged 18 to 19 in 1984. The rates for black women decreased by 35, 31 and 36 percent respectively from 1970 to 1982.

The birth rates for teens aged 10 to 14 are low and remained fairly stable throughout this period. However, for black teenagers this age, the birth rate has been at least seven times higher than the rate for white teenagers in all years.

TABLE 6.3 Number Of Out-Of-Wedlock Births In The United States (estimated) By Age Of Mother: 1955-1984 (females under 20, by race)

Year	All Races			Whites			Nonwhites			Blacks*		
	Under 15	15-17	18-19	Under 15	15-17	18-19	Under 15	15-17	18-19	Under 15	15-17	18-19
1984	9,075	115,355	145,749	3,193	57,980	75,295	5,882	57,375	70,454	5,634	54,062	65,680
1983	8,816	116,625	144,635	3,222	58,132	74,362	5,594	58,493	70,273	5,354	55,191	65,755
1982	8,720	117,696	142,930	3,225	57,848	72,829	5,495	59,848	70,101	5,305	56,608	65,555
1981	8,589	118,608	140,631	3,030	57,881	71,105	5,559	60,727	69,526	5,361	57,882	65,601
1980	9,024	121,900	140,877	3,144	57,761	70,223	5,880	64,139	70,654	5,707	61,204	66,818
1979	9,500	120,000	133,000	3,300	54,300	62,100	6,200	65,900	70,900	6,100	62,900	67,100
1978	9,400	116,500	123,200	3,300	52,500	55,900	6,100	64,000	67,300	5,900	61,200	64,000
1977	10,100	120,900	118,700	3,400	53,800	53,200	6,700	67,100	65,500	6,500	64,400	62,700
1976	10,300	116,500	108,500	3,400	53,800	47,600	6,800	66,500	60,900	6,600	64,100	58,600
1975	11,000	116,800	105,800	3,600	50,000	45,000	7,500	67,900	60,700	7,200	65,500	58,200
1974	10,600	113,000	97,700	3,300	48,900	40,300	7,300	68,300	57,500	7,700	66,100	55,100
1973	10,900	111,300	93,500	3,200	44,800	38,700	7,700	69,000	54,800	7,500	67,000	52,900
1972	9,900	108,500	93,700	2,700	42,400	38,700	7,200	68,600	55,100	7,100	66,700	53,200
1971	9,500	100,800	93,200	2,500	39,900	39,900	7,100	64,700	53,500	6,900	63,100	51,800
1970	9,500	96,100	94,300	2,500	36,200	43,200	7,000	60,000	51,100	6,800	58,400	49,500
1969	8,300	83,300	84,900	2,100	30,800	39,500	6,200	52,500	45,300	6,100	51,200	43,800
1968	7,700	77,900	80,200	1,900	28,400	38,900	5,800	49,500	41,200			
1967	6,900	70,900	73,500	1,700	24,800	35,500	5,200	46,100	38,000			
1966	6,200	65,900	69,800	1,400	23,400	34,100	4,800	42,500	35,800			
1965	6,100	61,700	61,400	1,400	21,500	29,200	4,600	40,200	32,200			
1964	5,800	58,700	52,700	1,400	21,600	23,600	4,400	37,100	29,100			
1963	5,400	51,100	50,700	1,200	17,900	21,900	4,000	31,800	27,500			
1962	5,100	46,100	48,300	1,300	15,500	20,700	3,800	29,700	26,600			
1961	5,200	45,100	48,100	1,400	15,500	20,600	3,800	29,600	27,500			
1960	4,600	43,700	43,400	1,200	15,000	17,800	3,500	28,700	25,600			
1959	4,600	43,100	41,500	1,200	14,400	16,500	3,400	28,600	25,000			
1958	4,400	40,100	39,300	1,200	13,200	15,300	3,300	26,900	24,000			
1957	4,600	39,400	37,100	1,100	12,500	14,400	3,500	26,900	22,700			
1956	4,200	37,000	35,900	1,000	11,400	13,900	3,200	25,600	22,000			
1955	3,900	34,700	34,200	900	10,600	13,100	3,000	24,200	21,100			

*Data for Blacks separately are not available prior to 1969.

Source: National Center for Health Statistics, Vital Statistics of the United States, annual volumes; See Table 6.1.

TABLE 6.3

Table 6.3 shows the total estimated number of out-of-wedlock births for mothers under age 20 from 1955 to 1984. Data are from the National Center for Health Statistics (NCHS).

In general, there was a rise in the number of out of wedlock births to women under age 20 from 1955 to 1984. Among white women, the number of out of wedlock births to women under age 15 rose in 1975 to 3,600 and then declined to 3,225 births in 1981. Out-of-wedlock births to women 15 to 17 and 18 to 19 rose in number throughout this period. There were over five times as many births to single white women in 1984 as in 1955, (10,600 compared to 57,848 for women aged 15 to 17 and 13,100 compared to 72,829 for women aged 18 to 19).

The number of out-of-wedlock births to nonwhite women under age 20 was generally higher than the number to whites; however the magnitude of the difference has declined over time. In 1955, white women less than 15 years of age had 70 percent fewer out of wedlock births than nonwhite women, 900 compared to 3,000 births. By 1984, white women under age 15 had about 46 percent fewer out of wedlock births than non white women, 3,193 versus 5,882 births. The decline in the difference between the number of births to nonwhite and white single women aged 15 to 17 and 18 to 19 was even more dramatic. There were 56 percent fewer births to single white women aged 15 to 17 compared to non-white women in 1955 and only 1 percent fewer in 1984. For women aged 18 to 19 there were 40 percent fewer out-of-wedlock births to whites than nonwhites in 1955, but 7 percent more out-of-wedlock births to whites than nonwhites in 1984.

Among black women, the number of out-of-wedlock births started to decline during the 1970's. The number of births to unmarried black women under age 15 declined 27 percent between the peak in 1974 and 1984, (7,700 compared to 5,634) births. The number of out-of-wedlock births to black women aged 15 to 17 declined by 19 percent from the 1973 peak to 1984, (67,000 to 54,062 births). The number of births to single black women aged 18 to 19 declined by about 2 percent from the peak in 1979 to 1984, (67,100 to 65,680 births).

TABLE 6.4 Birth Rates For Unmarried Women by Age of Mother and Race of Child: United States, 1970-84 (rates are live births to unmarried women per 1,000 unmarried women in specified group, estimated as of July 1)

Years and Race of Child	Total	Age of Mother	
		15-19 Years	
		15-17 Years	18-19 Years
All Races			
1984	30.2	21.9	43.0
1983	29.7	22.1	41.0
1982	28.9	21.5	40.2
1981	28.2	20.9	39.9
1980	27.6	20.6	39.0
1979	26.4	19.9	37.2
1978	24.9	19.1	35.1
1977	25.1	19.8	34.6
1976	23.7	19.0	32.1
1975	23.9	19.3	32.5
1974	23.0	18.8	31.2
1973	22.7	18.7	30.4
1972	22.8	18.5	30.9
1971	22.3	17.5	31.7
1970	22.4	17.1	32.9
White			
1984	19.0	13.5	27.6
1983	18.5	13.5	26.1
1982	17.7	12.9	25.1
1981	17.1	12.4	24.6
1980	16.2	11.8	23.6
1979	14.6	10.8	21.0
1978	13.6	10.3	19.3
1977	13.4	10.5	18.7
1976	12.3	9.7	16.9
1975	12.0	9.6	16.5
1974	11.0	8.8	15.3
1973	10.6	8.4	14.9
1972	10.4	8.0	15.1
1971	10.3	7.4	15.8
1970	10.9	7.5	17.0

TABLE 6.4 (contineud)

Years and Race of Child	Total	Age of Mother	
		15-19 Years	
		15-17 Years	18-19 Years
All Other			
1984	78.3	59.3	106.1
1983	78.3	60.2	104.6
1982	79.2	60.7	107.0
1981	79.2	60.3	109.0
1980	81.7	63.1	111.6
1979	83.9	64.8	115.3
1978	81.2	63.2	111.6
1977	84.0	67.2	112.7
1976	82.5	67.5	108.9
1975	86.3	70.7	114.3
1974	87.3	73.2	113.4
1973	88.5	75.6	112.8
1972	91.8	77.6	119.3
1971	92.0	75.4	125.4
1970	90.8	73.3	126.5
Black			
1984	87.1	66.8	116.2
1983	86.4	67.1	114.0
1982	87.0	67.6	115.8
1981	86.8	66.9	117.6
1980	89.2	69.6	120.2
1979	91.0	71.0	123.3
1978	87.9	68.8	119.6
1977	90.9	73.0	121.7
1976	89.7	73.5	117.9
1975	93.5	76.8	123.8
1974	93.8	78.6	122.2
1973	94.9	81.2	120.5
1972	98.2	82.8	128.2
1971	98.6	80.7	135.2
1970	96.9	77.9	136.4

Source: NCHS <u>Advanced Reported of Natality Statistics 1984</u>, <u>Monthly Vital Statistics Report</u>, Vol 35, No. 4, July 1986.

TABLE 6.4

Table 6.4 presents birth rates for unmarried women by age and race for 1970 to 1984. For all women age 15 to 19, out-of-wedlock birth rates rose from 22.4 births in 1970 to 30.2 births per 1,000 women in 1984, a 34.8 percent increase. The increase in out-of-wedlock birth rates was slightly larger for women age 15 to 17 than for women age 18 to 19, a 28.1 and 30.7 percent increase respectively. Throughout this period, however, out-of-wedlock birth rates for women age 18 to 19 were almost double the rates for women age 15 to 17. In 1984, the out-of-wedlock birth rate was 21.9 births per 1,000 unmarried 15 to 17 year old women compared to 43.0 births per 1,000 unmarried 18 to 19 year old women.

The overall increase in out-of-wedlock birth rates for women age 15 to 19 was due to increased rates of out-of-wedlock child-bearing among white adolescents. The birth rate for unmarried white women aged 15 to 19 rose from 10.9 to 19.0 births per 1,000 unmarried women from 1970 to 1984, a 74 percent increase. For nonwhite and black unmarried women, the birth rates fell from 90.8 to 78.3 and 96.9 to 87.1 births per 1,000 unmarried women, decreases of 14 and 11 percent respectively.

Despite this trend, there were consistently more out-of-wedlock births per 1,000 unmarried nonwhite teenage women than per 1,000 white women. In 1984, there were 13.5 out-of-wedlock births to white women age 15 to 17 compared to 59.3 per 1,000 nonwhite women. For women age 18 to 19 there were 27.6 births per 1,000 white women compared to 106.1 per 1,000 nonwhite women.

TABLE 6.5 Live Births By Age Of Father, Age Of Mother, And Race Of Child: United States, 1984 (based on 100 percent of births in 46 states and on a 50-percent sample of births in four states and the District of Columbia)

Age of Mother And Race of Child	Total	Age of Father										Not Stated	Total Reported
		>15 Years	15-19 Years	20-24 Years	25-29 Years	30-34 Years	35-39 Years	40-44 Years	45-49 Years	50-54 Years	55+ Years		
All Races[1]													
All ages	3,669,141	232	109,032	696,207	1,067,147	805,875	355,843	109,468	32,044	11,298	7,092	474,903	3,178,241
Under 15 years	9,965	84	2,088	698	113	28	7	5	2	--	6	6,934	2,967
15-19 years	469,682	113	87,179	167,940	34,011	6,976	2,107	770	257	117	83	170,129	317,329
20-24 years	1,141,578	10	18,123	445,701	381,915	89,465	23,859	7,198	2,210	895	671	171,531	994,817
25-29 years	1,165,711	13	1,330	70,235	562,980	341,880	80,390	20,411	5,863	2,128	1,377	79,104	1,074,015
30-34 years	658,496	9	260	9,836	78,103	332,500	156,177	34,113	9,123	3,243	1,956	33,176	594,353
35-39 years	195,755	3	47	1,610	9,233	33,032	88,689	36,863	9,479	3,130	1,979	11,690	169,943
40-44 years	26,846	--	5	177	770	1,956	4,543	9,934	4,739	1,575	922	2,225	23,777
45-49 years	1,108	--	--	10	22	38	71	174	371	210	98	114	1,040
White													
All ages	2,923,502	104	83,206	580,835	918,970	689,253	298,184	87,662	24,147	8,114	4,768	228,259	2,685,457
Under 15 years	3,959	27	1,014	513	77	19	5	4	2	--	--	2,298	1,643
15-19 years	320,953	59	66,154	136,601	27,477	5,500	1,683	581	201	74	52	82,571	255,022
20-24 years	898,919	5	14,701	375,941	324,933	72,976	19,184	5,502	1,598	629	442	83,008	839,134
25-29 years	969,061	8	1,084	58,350	492,679	291,309	65,709	16,096	4,236	1,445	889	37,256	922,541
30-34 years	549,595	5	211	7,952	65,751	290,289	132,049	27,079	6,847	2,300	1,266	15,846	506,229
35-39 years	159,246	--	37	1,315	7,418	27,566	75,803	30,119	7,236	2,325	1,390	6,037	141,581
40-44 years	20,974	--	5	156	618	1,564	3,701	8,143	3,744	1,196	664	1,183	18,990
45-49 years	795	--	--	7	17	30	50	138	283	145	65	60	752

TABLE 5.5 (continued)

Age of Mother And Race of Child	Total	Age of Father ≥15 Years	15-19 Years	20-24 Years	25-29 Years	30-34 Years	35-39 Years	40-44 Years	45-49 Years	50-54 Years	55+ Years	Not Stated	Total Reported
Black													
All Ages	592,745	112	22,351	93,273	109,943	75,722	35,918	14,377	5,565	2,295	1,646	231,543	358,329
Under 15 years	5,720	56	1,012	145	34	7	2	1	--	--	5	4,458	1,207
15-19 years	134,392	45	18,373	26,244	5,099	1,117	341	151	54	39	30	82,899	52,266
20-24 years	203,562	5	2,745	56,618	43,783	11,646	3,426	1,345	490	224	173	83,107	121,198
25-29 years	147,111	3	189	8,829	51,429	32,832	9,407	3,129	1,253	526	381	39,133	106,524
30-34 years	73,858	2	30	1,245	8,322	26,571	14,502	4,525	1,629	666	480	15,886	56,070
35-39 years	24,028	1	2	176	1,177	3,305	7,723	4,099	1,461	574	401	5,109	17,801
40-44 years	3,906	--	--	16	96	237	507	1,108	637	233	165	907	3,108
45-49 years	168	--	--	--	3	7	10	19	41	33	11	44	155

[1]Includes races other than White and Black.

Source: NCHS, "Advanced Report of Natality Statistics 1983," *Monthly Vital Statistics Report*, Vol. 35, No. 4, July 1986.

TABLE 6.5

Table 6.5 presents data on the number of live births by the age of father, age of mother and the race of the child for 1984.

Caution should be used when interpreting this table because the distribution of the age of father by the age of the mother among those not reporting is not known. About 70 percent of mothers under age 15 and 36 percent of mothers age 15 to 19 did not report the age of the father. Among white teenagers 58 percent of those under age 15 and about 26 percent of those aged 15 to 19 did not report the age of the father of their child. Among black teenagers, 78 percent of those under age 15 and 62 percent of those aged 15 to 19 did not report the age of the father of their child. These data are from the National Center for Health Statistics (NCHS).

This table shows that the majority of women under age 20 giving birth and reporting the age of the father have partners older than themselves. Nearly all women under age 15, 97 percent, had partners aged 15 or over and 28 percent had partners over age 19. Among mothers aged 15 to 19, 71 percent had partners over age 19 and 15 percent had partners over age 24.

White teenage mothers are more likely to report having older partners than black mothers. Among white mothers under age 15, 37 percent reported having partners over age 19. In comparison, among black mothers under age 15, 15 percent reported having partners over age 19. Among both black and white women aged 15 to 19 reporting the father's age, 72 percent of the white mothers aged 15 to 19 had partners over age 24 compared to 64 percent of the black mothers aged 15 to 19.

TABLE 6.5 Percent Of All First Births And Total Births In Which The Mother's Age Was Under 20, Under 18 Or Under 15, By Race, United States, 1950-1984

Age of Mother	All Races*						White						Black**					
	First Births			All Births			First Births			All Births			First Births			All Births		
Year	<15	≤17	<20	<15	≤17	<20	<15	≤17	<20	<15	≤17	<20	<15	≤17	<20	<15	≤17	<20
1984	0.6	10	24	0.3	5	13	0.3	8	21	0.1	4	11	2	22	44	1.0	11	24
1983	0.6	10	25	0.3	5	14	0.3	8	22	0.1	4	12	2	23	45	0.9	11	24
1982	0.6	11	26	0.3	5	14	0.3	8	23	0.1	4	12	2	23	45	0.9	11	25
1981	0.6	11	27	0.3	5	15	0.3	9	24	0.1	4	13	2	24	46	1	11	25
1980	0.6	11	28	0.3	6	16	0.3	9	25	0.1	5	14	2	26	48	1	12	26
1975	0.9	16	35	0.4	8	19	0.5	13	31	0.2	6	16	3	32	57	1	16	33
1970	0.7	14	36	0.3	6	18	0.3	11	32	0.1	5	15	3	32	59	1	15	31
1965	0.6	14	38	0.2	5	16	0.2	11	35	0.1	4	14	3	33	59	0.9	12	22
1960	0.6	14	37	0.2	4	14	0.3	12	34	0.1	4	13	3	30	54	0.6	9	20
1955	0.5	12	31	0.1	4	12	0.2	9	28	0.1	3	11	3	28	51	0.6	8	20
1950	0.4	10	27	0.1	4	12	0.2	8	24	0.1	3	10	3	28	50	0.7	9	21

*Includes races other than white and black.

**Percentages for the years 1950, 1955 and 1960 pertain to non-whites rather than blacks due to insufficient data on live black births.

Source: National Center for Health Statistics, calculated from Vital Statistics of the United States, annual volumes; NCHS "Advanced Final Natality Report", Monthly Vital Statistics Report, Vol. 34, No. 6, September 1985 and Vol. 35, No. 4, July 1986.

TABLE 6.6

The percent of all first births and total births in which the mother's age was under 20, under 18 or under 15, by race, is shown in Table 6.6.

Data are from the National Center for Health Statistics (NCHS). There are four important points to make about these data. First, the proportion of first births to women under age 20 is consistently higher than the percent of all births to women under age 20. Second, both proportions are due not only to the rate of childbearing among teens, but the birth rates of older women and to the size of population groups below and above age 20. Third, there was an increase in the proportion of first births and all births to women under age 20 from 1950 to the early 1970s. By 1984 the percent of first births to women under age 20 had declined; but the percent of all births to women under age 20 remained higher than in 1950. Fourth, black teens under age 20 consistently made up a larger proportion of both the first births and all births to black women than white teens under age 20 did among whites. Just under half of all black first-born children has a mother not yet 20 years of age.

TABLE 6.7 Number and Percent of All Live Births to Women Under Age 20 by Hispanic Origin of Mother: Total of 23 Reporting States and the District of Columbia, 1984

		Mother of Hispanic Origin						
Age of Mother	All Origins	Total	Mexican	Puerto Rican	Cuban	Central And South American	Other	Non-Hispanic	Not Stated
All ages	2,230,815	346,986	225,767	34,219	9,477	36,401	41,122	1,791,949	91,880
	(100.0)	(100.0)	(100.0)	(100.0)	(100.0)	(100.0)	(100.0)	(100.0)	(100.0)
Under 15	6,318	1,242	860	179	9	34	160	4,830	246
	(0.3)	(0.4)	(0.4)	(0.5)	(0.1)	(0.1)	(0.4)	(0.3)	(0.3)
15-19 years	288,346	57,717	39,712	7,112	766	2,930	7,197	218,930	11,699
	(12.9)	(16.6)	(17.6)	(20.8)	(8.1)	(8.0)	(17.5)	(12.2)	(12.7)
15 years	15,217	3,300	2,322	366	25	119	468	11,355	562
	(0.7)	(1.0)	(1.0)	(1.1)	(0.3)	(0.3)	(1.1)	(0.6)	(0.6)
16 years	33,080	7,239	5,127	877	73	251	911	24,530	1,311
	(1.5)	(2.1)	(2.3)	(2.6)	(0.8)	(0.7)	(2.2)	(1.4)	(1.4)
17 years	54,817	11,395	7,961	1,493	128	467	1,347	41,125	2,297
	(2.5)	(3.3)	(3.5)	(4.4)	(1.4)	(1.3)	(3.3)	(2.3)	(2.5)
18 years	79,502	15,909	10,851	2,014	208	858	1,978	60,437	3,236
	(3.6)	(4.6)	(4.8)	(5.9)	(2.2)	(2.4)	(4.8)	(3.4)	(3.5)
19 years	105,650	19,874	13,451	2,363	332	1,235	2,493	81,483	4,293
	(4.7)	(5.7)	(6.0)	(6.9)	(3.5)	(3.4)	(6.1)	(4.5)	(4.7)

Note: Data are for births to residents of the 23 states and the District of Columbia reporting ethnic of Hispanic origin, regardless of where the births occurred. Births occurring in non-reporting states to residents of the 23 reporting states are included in the "not stated" category.

Percentages do not total to 100.0 because births to women ages 20 and over are not shown. Approximately 4 percent of all mothers did not report their ethnicity as Hispanic or non Hispanic.

Source: Unpublished tabulations from the Division of Vital Statistics, National Center for Health Statistics, January 27, 1986.

TABLE 6.7

Table 6.7 presents the number and percent of all live births to women under age 20 by Hispanic origin of mother for 1984. Data are from the National Center for Health Statistics (NCHS).

These data indicate that of all births to adolescent mothers of Hispanic origin most are to mothers of Mexican origin. There were 39,712 births to mothers of Mexican origin aged 15 to 19 compared to 7,112 births to Puerto Rican mothers aged 15 to 19, 2,930 births to Central and South American mothers aged 15 to 19 and 766 to Cuban mothers aged 15 to 19.

Births to women under age 20 constituted 17 percent of births to all Hispanic origin mothers compared to 13.2 percent of births to non-Hispanic mothers in these states. Among mothers of Hispanic origin, births to Puerto Rican women aged 15 to 19 made up 21.3 percent of all births to Puerto Rican mothers and births to women under age 20 made up 18.0 percent of all births to Mexican mothers.

TABLE 6.8 Number and Percent of All Out of Wedlock Births to Women Under Age 20 by Hispanic Origin of Mother: Total of 23 Reporting States and the District of Columbia, 1984

		Mother of Hispanic Origin					
Age of Mother	All Origins	Total	Mexican	Puerto Rican	Cuban	Central And South American	Other	Non-Hispanic	Not Stated
All Ages	489,400	98,273	54,617	17,397	1,534	12,381	12,350	372,586	18,541
	(100.0)	(100.0)	(100.0)	(100.0)	(100.0)	(100.0)	(100.0)	(100.0)	(100.0)
Under 15	5,688	972	617	177	9	33	136	4,494	222
	(1.2)	(1.0)	(1.1)	(1.0)	(0.6)	(0.3)	(1.1)	(1.2)	(1.2)
15-19	160,500	28,577	17,103	5,179	288	1,704	4,303	125,712	6,211
	(32.8)	(29.1)	(31.3)	(29.8)	(18.8)	(13.8)	(34.8)	(33.7)	(33.5)
15-17	70,863	12,957	8,099	2,217	112	587	1,942	55,123	2,783
	(14.5)	(13.2)	(14.8)	(12.7)	(7.3)	(4.7)	(15.7)	(14.8)	(15.0)
18-19	89,637	15,620	9,004	2,962	176	1,117	2,361	70,589	3,428
	(18.3)	(15.9)	(16.5)	(17.0)	(11.5)	(9.1)	(19.1)	(18.9)	(18.5)

Note: Data are for births to residents of the 23 states and the District of Columbia regardless of where the births occurred. Births occurring in non-reporting states to residents of the 23 reporting states are included in the "non-stated" category.
Approximately 4 percent of all mothers did not report their ethnicity as Hispanic or non-Hispanic.

Source: Unpublished tabulations from the Division of Vital Statistics, National Center for Health Statistics, January 27, 1986.

TABLE 6.8

Table 6.8 presents the number and percent of all out-of-wedlock births to women under age 20 by Hispanic origin of mother for 1984. Data are from the National Center for Health Statistics (NCHS).

These data indicate that the largest number of out-of-wedlock births to adolescent women of Hispanic origin was to Mexican women. There were 28,577 out-of-wedlock births to Hispanic mothers aged 15 to 19 in 1984; 17,103 of those births were to Mexican women aged 15 to 19.

Out-of-wedlock births made up 10 percent of all births to Hispanic women aged 15 to 19. In addition, Hispanic women aged 15 to 19 accounted for 18 percent of all nonmarital births in this age group.

Overall, out-of-wedlock births to non-Hispanic women aged 15 to 19 accounted for a slightly larger proportion of all out-of-wedlock births among non-Hispanics than among Hispanics, 33.7 percent compared to 29.1 percent respectively.

TABLE 6.9 Percentage Of Mothers Receiving Inadequate Prenatal Care (third trimester only or no care), By Age Group According To Race And Ethnicity, Residence And Marital Status, National Natality Survey 1980

	Age Group		
	<20	20-24	25
Total	9.8	4.9	2.9
Race/Ethnicity			
Black (non-Hispanic)	12.8	6.4	3.6
White (non-Hispanic)	8.3	3.9	2.5
Hispanic	11.9	11.4	6.4
Residence			
Metropolitan	10.3	4.8	2.7
Non-metropolitan	8.9	5.3	3.4
Marital Status			
Married	5.0	3.4	2.5
Unmarried	14.8	11.4	7.0

Source: S. Singh, A. Torres and J.D. Forrest, "The Need for Prenatal Care in the United States: Evidence from the 1980 National Natality Survey", Family Planning Perspectives, Vol. 17, No. 3, 1985.

TABLE 6.9

Table 6.9 shows the percentage of mothers receiving inadequate prenatal care (third trimester only or no care), by age group according to race and ethnicity, residence, and marital status. The data are from the 1980 National Natality Survey (NNS).

These data indicate that in 1980, 9.8 percent of all mothers under age 20 received inadequate prenatal care, compared to 4.9 percent of mothers aged 20 to 24 and 2.9 percent of mothers aged 25 and over. Black mothers under age 20 were the most likely to receive inadequate prenatal care, 12.8 percent compared to 11.9 percent of Hispanic and 8.3 percent of white mothers, even though Hispanic mothers of other ages were more likely than black or white women to receive inadequate care. Also, unmarried mothers of all ages were more likely than married mothers to have had inadequate prenatal care.

TABLE 6.10 Number and Percent Of Live Births With Low Birth Weight and Live Births by Birth Weight, by Age of Mother and Race of Child: United States, 1983; Based On 100 Percent Of Births In Selected States And On A 50-percent Sample Of Births In All Other States

Age of Mother and Race of Child	Low Birth Weight[1] Number	Low Birth Weight[1] Percent	Total
All Races			
All ages	246,105	6.7	3,669,141
Under 15 years	1,350	13.6	9,965
15-19 years	43,817	9.3	469,682
15 years	2,744	11.4	24,142
16 years	5,789	10.9	53,178
17 years	8,719	9.8	89,424
18 years	12,087	9.3	130,159
19 years	14,478	8.4	172,779
20-24 years	78,444	6.9	1,141,578
25-29 years	68,224	5.9	1,165,711
30-34 years	38,762	5.9	658,496
35-39 years	13,180	6.7	195,755
40-44 years	2,220	8.3	26,846
45-49 years	108	9.8	1,108
White			
All ages	163,117	5.6	2,923,502
Under 15 years	428	10.8	3,959
15-19 years	24,503	7.6	320,953
15 years	1,187	9.2	12,869
16 years	2,981	9.2	32,529
17 years	4,794	8.1	59,618
18 years	6,968	7.7	90,470
19 years	8,573	6.8	125,467
20-24 years	51,122	5.7	898,919
25-29 years	48,138	5.0	969,061
30-34 years	28,013	5.1	549,595
35-39 years	9,302	5.9	159,246
40-44 years	1,540	7.4	20,974
45-49 years	71	9.0	795
All Other			
All ages	82,988	11.1	745,639
Under 15 years	922	15.4	6,006
15-19 years	19,314	13.0	148,729
15 years	1,557	13.8	11,273
16 years	2,808	13.6	20,649
17 years	3,925	13.2	29,806
18 years	5,119	12.9	39,689
19 years	5,905	12.5	47,312
20-24 years	27,322	11.3	242,659
25-29 years	20,086	10.2	196,650
30-34 years	10,749	9.9	108,901
35-39 years	3,878	10.6	36,509
40-44 years	680	11.6	5,872
45-49 years	37	11.9	313
Black			
All ages	73,178	12.4	592,745
Under 15 years	891	15.6	5,720
15-19 years	18,147	13.5	134,392
15 years	1,501	14.1	10,637
16 years	2,678	14.0	19,158
17 years	3,703	13.7	27,112
18 years	4,782	13.4	35,656
19 years	5,483	13.1	41,829
20-24 years	24,699	12.2	203,562
25-29 years	17,231	11.7	147,111
30-34 years	8,640	11.7	73,858
35-39 years	3,018	12.6	24,028
40-44 years	530	13.6	3,906
45-49 years	22	13.1	168

[1] Less than 2,500 grams.

Sources: NCHS, "Advanced Final Natality by Statistics, 1983", Monthly Vital Statistics Report, Vol. 35, No. 4, July 1986.

TABLE 6.10

Table 6.10 shows the number and percent of babies with low birth weight by age and race of mother in 1984. Data are from the National Center for Health Statistics.

In general, mothers less than age 20 and aged 40 to 49 were more likely than women aged 20 to 39 to have babies with low birth weights. Over 13 percent of the babies born to women under age 15 had low birth rates, more than 9 percent of those born to women aged 15 to 19, 8.3 percent of those born to women aged 40 to 44, and almost 10 percent born to women aged 45 to 49.

Black babies born to mothers of all ages were more likely to have low birth weights than white babies. About 6 percent of all white babies had low birth weights compared to over 11 percent of all black babies. Over 10 percent of the white babies born to teens less than age 15 and 7.6 percent of the white babies born to teens aged 15 to 19 had low birth weights compared to 15.4 percent of black babies born to teens under age 15 and 13.0 percent of those born to teens aged 15 to 19.

TABLE 6.11 Estimated Cumulative Percent of Women Aged 15 to 19 Ever Experiencing A First Birth By Single Year of Age, Race And Ethnicity*, 1982 National Survey of Family Growth

Age[1]	Cumulative Percent Having a First Birth
Total Sample	
15	0.2
16	3.2
17	5.5
18	12.0
19	17.1
N 1888	
Whites	
15	--
16	2.2
17	3.3
18	10.7
19	13.2
N 1253	
Blacks	
15	1.2
16	7.8
17	15.5
18	20.3
19	39.8
N 581	
Hispanics	
15	--
16	--
17	5.1
18	29.6
19	47.0
N 159	

--Cell sizes were less than 20.

*Hispanic persons may be of any race, and whites and blacks may include Hispanic persons.

[1]Single years of age refer to the midpoints in the age intervals, e.g., 15 means 15.5 years.

Source: Special tabulations from the 1982 National Survey of Family Growth, conducted by the National Center for Health Statistics, DHHS.

TABLE 6.11

Table 6.11 presents the estimated cumulative percent of women aged 15 to 19 ever experiencing a first birth by age, race and ethnicity. The data are from the 1982 National Survey of Family Growth (NSFG).

These data indicate that among all women, 17.1 percent had a first birth before age 20. The estimated proportion of women having a first birth before age 20 was the highest for Hispanic women, 47.0 percent, compared to 39.8 percent for black women and 13.2 percent for white women. Most of these births occur at ages 18 and 19. At age 17, blacks are 3 times more likely than Hispanic women to have had a birth.

TABLE 6.12 Cumulative Percent Having A First Birth By Single Year Of Age, Race And Ethnicity[1], And By Mother's Education, Education in 1979; 1983 National Longitudinal Survey of Youth

	Total Sample					
	Males			Females		
	Respondent's Mother's Education					
Age*	<HS	=HS	≥HS	<HS	=HS	≥HS
Total Sample						
15	.1	.1	0	.7	.3	.1
16	.4	.2	.1	3.4	.9	.2
17	1.2	.6	.1	9.1	2.9	1.6
18	3.1	1.4	.5	16.5	6.0	2.5
19	6.5	3.2	1.0	24.3	10.2	5.2
20	11.7	5.8	2.7	34.6	16.0	7.5
N	1808	1878	790	1975	1791	756
Whites						
15	0	0	0	.5	.2	0
16	.2	0	0	2.1	.7	0
17	.4	.2	0	6.4	2.1	1.1
18	2.0	.6	.3	13.1	4.4	1.7
19	4.5	2.1	.6	19.8	8.3	4.3
20	9.1	4.8	2.1	30.9	13.9	6.3
N	814	1359	592	833	1288	577
	<HS		≥HS	<HS		≥HS
Blacks						
15	.6		.7	1.6		.9
16	1.0		1.5	7.5		2.7
17	4.0		3.5	17.9		9.2
18	7.0		5.8	27.3		17.0
19	11.9		10.4	38.2		22.3
20	18.4		13.1	47.1		28.5
N	541		525	595		499
Hispanics						
15	--		--	.4		--
16	.4		--	3.2		.7
17	.6		.4	8.2		.7
18	2.8		2.8	16.3		3.7
19	7.6		4.6	23.9		11.7
20	14.2		6.1	33.1		18.9
N	453		192	496		183

*Percentages refer to birthday for specified ages, e.g., 15 means by 15th birthday or by end of age 14.

[1] Hispanic Persons may be of any race.

Note: Sample is limited to respondents age 20 and over at 1983 survey date.

Source: Special Tabulations from the 1983 National Longitidunal Survey of Youth, Center for Human Resource Research, Ohio State University.

TABLE 6.12

Table 6.12 displays the cumulative percent reporting a first birth by mother's education. Data are from the 1983 National Longitudinal Survey of Youth (NLS).

Males were less likely than females to report having a child by age 20, despite the higher percent of males than females who were sexually active by age 20. Also, blacks were more likely than whites or hispanics to report a first birth by age 20 regardless of their mother's education. In general, however, adolescent males whose mothers had less than high school educations were more likely to have child by age 20 than those whose mother's education was high school or more. Of all males, the proportion with a child was about 12 percent among those whose mother's education was less than high school, less than 6 percent among those whose mothers had completed high school, and less than 3 percent among males whose mothers had gone beyond high school education.

Among the females, the proportion reporting a birth by age 20 was about 35 percent among those whose mother's education was less than high school, 16 percent of those whose mothers had a high school education and 8 percent among those whose mothers had more than a high school education. Blacks were more likely to report having a birth, regardless of the mother's education.

TABLE 6.13 Infant Mortality Rates (deaths at less one year of age per 1,000 live births) By Age Of Mother, U.S. 1960 Study Of Infant Mortality From Linked Records And 1980 National Natality Survey/National Death Index (NNS/NDI)

Age of Mother	1960 Study of Linked Records	1980 NNS/NDI		
	Rate	Rate	Standard Error	Percent Decline
Under 20 years	33.1	17.4	2.4	47.4
20-24	24.2	12.5	1.3	48.3
25-29	22.4	9.8	1.3	56.3
30-34	23.7	14.7	2.5	38.0
35+ years	26.7	18.4*	7.7	31.1

*Infant mortality rates based on less than 30 sample cases do not meet standards of reliability or precision.

Source: K.G. Keppel, P.J. Placek, G.A. Simpson and S.S. Kessel "Infant Mortality Rates from the 1980 National Natality Survey and Twenty Year Trend Comparisons" NCHS, Unpublished paper, 1985.

TABLE 6.13

Table 6.13 presents infant mortality rates by age of mother for 1960 and 1980. The 1960 data are from the Study of Infant Mortality From Linked Records and the 1980 data are from the National Natality Survey/National Death Index.

These data indicate that in 1960 mothers under age 20 had the highest infant mortality rate, 33.1 infant deaths per 1,000 live births. In 1980, the infant mortality rate for mothers under age 20 was 17.4 deaths per 1,000 births, a 47.4 percent decline. The infant mortality rates in 1980 for mothers under age 20 were still higher than for mothers aged 20 to 34, despite the overall decline in U.S. infant mortality rates. The rate for mothers over age 35 is based on too few cases to be a reliable estimate.

VII. ADOPTION OF CHILDREN BORN TO ADOLESCENTS

This section presents information on adolescent placement for adoption of premarital births, by age and race of the mother. There is no national system for the collection of data on adoptions or the characteristics of mothers who relinquish children for adoption. The data presented here are from the National Survey of Family Growth, National Survey of Young Women (NSYW), and the State of California. Problems with these data include under-reporting and incomplete information on characteristics of the mothers relinquishing children for adoption. These data, however, do demonstrate the declining tendency of adolescents to give up a child born out of wedlock.

TABLE 7.1 Percentage Distribution Of Premarital Live Births Resulting From First Pregnancies Of Women Aged 15-19 At Interview, By Living Arrangements Of Baby And Race Of Mother: 1982, 1976, and 1971

Percentage Distribution

Living Arrangements Of Baby	All Races			White and Other			Black		
	1982	1976	1971	1982	1976	1971	1982	1976	1971
All Births (number in sample)	133	148	259	50	25	39	83	123	220
Total	100.0	100.0	100.0	100.0	100.0	100.0	100.0	100.0	100.0
In mother's household	92.6	93.3	85.6	91.1	87.2	72.2	94.7	96.8	92.4
With relatives or friends[a]	2.5	1.0	4.7	1.5	2.9	5.8	4.0	0.0	4.2
Adopted	4.6	2.6	7.6	7.4	7.0	18.4	0.7	0.0	2.0
No longer living	0.3	3.1	2.1	0.0	2.9	3.6	0.6	3.2	1.4

[a] "Friends" was a valid code in the 1971 and 1976 surveys, but not in the 1982 survey.

Source: C.A. Bachrach, "Adoption Plans, Adopted Children, and Adopted Mothers", Journal of Marriage and the Family, 48 (May 1986): 243 - 253. Reprinted by permission.

TABLE 7.1

Table 7.1 shows the percentage distribution of premarital live births resulting from first pregnancies to women aged 15 to 19 by the living arrangements of baby and the race of the mother for 1982, 1976, and 1971. It should be noted that under-reporting is presumed on survey questions concerning relinquishment for adoption; however, the extent of under-reporting cannot be estimated in the absence of data from any other reporting system. The data for 1976 and 1971 are from the National Surveys of Young Women. The 1982 data are from the 1982 National Survey of Family Growth. (NSFG)

Among women of all races the proportion of women aged 15 to 19 reporting that the child resulting from their first premarital pregnancy was adopted was lower in 1982 than in 1971, 4.6 percent in 1982 compared to 7.6 percent in 1971. Among white and other women (nonblack women) aged 15 to 19, the proportion declined from 18.4 percent in 1971 to 7.4 percent in 1982. Among black women aged 15 to 19 the proportion declined from 2 percent in 1971 to less than 1 percent in 1982.

TABLE 7.2 Percentage Of Babies Born Premaritally To Women 15-44 Years Of Age At Interview Who Were Placed For Adoption By Age Of Mother At Birth Of Child And Race, 1982 National Survey of Family Growth

	Percentage Placed for Adoption		
	All Races	White	Black
All Births	6.2 (N=8,455)	12.2 (N=3,886)	0.4 (N=4,426)
Age of Mother at Birth			
17 or younger	8.1	17.2	1.0
18-19	4.6	10.1	0.0
20-44	5.9	10.9	0.2
Year of Birth			
Before 1973	8.5	19.5	0.7
1973 or later	4.6	8.0	0.1

Source: C.A. Bachrach, "Adoptive Plans, Adopted Children, and Adopted Mothers", Journal of Marriage and the Family, 48 (May 1986): 243-253. Reprinted by permission.

TABLE 7.2

Table 7.2 shows the proportion of babies born to unmarried women (aged 15 to 44 at the date of the interview) who were placed for adoption by the age of the mother at the birth of the child according to race. (Again, it should be noted that under-reporting of adoption is likely.) Data are from the 1982 National Survey of Family Growth (NSFG).

A higher proportion of white women had placed a child born premaritally for adoption than black women, 12.2 percent compared to less than 1 percent. Among white women who were age 17 or younger at the birth of the child, 17.2 percent placed the child for adoption compared to 1 percent of black women who were age 17 or younger at the birth of the child.

Of women who had a premarital birth before 1973, 19.5 percent of the white women and .7 percent of black women placed the child for adoption. Of women who had a premarital birth during 1973 or later, 8 percent of the white women and .1 percent of the black women placed the child for adoption.

TABLE 7.3 Adoptions by Type* and Age of Mother, State of California Selected Years, 1967 to 1983

Year	Age of Mother	Number of Relinquishment[1] Adoptions	% of Total Relinquishment Adoptions	Number of Independent[2] Adoptions	% of Total Independent Adoptions
FY'1982-83	All Ages	1,831	100.0	1,534	100.0
	10-14	47	2.6	32	2.1
	15-16	165	9.0	159	11.0
	17-18	288	15.7	307	20.0
	<19	500	27.3	498	33.1
FY'1981-82	All Ages	1,991	100.0	1,534	100.0
	10-14	36	1.8	32	2.1
	15-16	204	10.2	169	11.0
	17-18	308	15.5	307	20.0
	<19	548	27.5	508	33.1
FY'1980-81	All Ages	1,937	100.0	n.a.	n.a.
	10-14	34	1.8		
	15-16	208	10.7		
	17-18	324	16.7		
	<19	566	29.2		
1979 (Jan-Dec)	All Ages	2,170	100.0	n.a.	n.a.
	10-14	50	2.3		
	15-19	857	39.5		
	<20	907	41.8		
1976 (Jan-Dec)	All Ages	2,251	100.0	n.a.	n.a.
	10-14	68	3.0		
	15-19	924	41.1		
	<20	992	44.1		
1975 (Jan-Dec)	All Ages	2,638	100.0	n.a.	n.a.
	10-14	62	2.4		
	15-19	1,133	42.8		
	<20	1,195	45.3		
1969 (Jan-Dec)	All Ages	8,151	100.0	n.a.	n.a.
	10-14	87	1.1		
	15-19	3,476	42.6		
	<20	3,563	43.7		
1967 (Jan-Dec)	All Ages	--	--	8,195	100.0
	10-14	n.a.	n.a.	n.a.	n.a.
	15-19	n.a.	n.a.	n.a.	n.a.
	<20	n.a.	n.a.	3,419	41.7

[1] Relinquishment is defined to include cases in which the child is turned over to a public or private adoption agency for placement.

[2] Independent adoptions are those in which the mother of the child arranges the adoption independent of or through an adoption agency. The data for independent adoptions are collected in survey form and the exact response rate is not known.

n.a. - not available.

*Foreign born adoptions are not included under either relinquishment or independent adoptions. Adoptions by relatives of the child are included in both totals and represent approximately 15 percent of the total number of adoptions for both categories although they are not tabulated separately from nonrelative adoptions.

Source: Program Information Series Reports; Department of Social Services, California, 1985.

TABLE 7.3

Table 7.3 shows the number and percentage distribution regarding relinquishment and independent adoptions by the age of the mother, for the State of California. Data on adoptions are collected by the Department of Social Services in California.

The important features of these data are the trends in the decreasing number of total adoptions and the declining proportion of adopted babies whose birth mothers were less than age 19 or 20. In 1969 there were 8,151 relinquishment adoptions and 3,563, or 44 percent, of those babies were born to mothers under age 20. In FY'1982-83, there were only 1,831 total relinquishment adoptions and only 500, or 27 percent of those babies were born to mothers less than age 19.

Although data are available for fewer years regarding independent adoptions, the same trend is evident. In 1967 there were 8,195 adoptions and 3,419, or 42 percent, of those babies were born to mothers less than age 20, while in FY'1982-83 there were only 1,534 independent adoptions and 498, or 33 percent, of those babies born to mothers under age 19.

VIII. ADOLESCENT PARENTS

This section presents information on characteristics of adolescent parents. Data on educational attainment, subsequent pregnancies, and social and economic status of the parents are shown. These data are from the 1983 National Longitudinal Survey (NLS) and 1982 National Survey of Family Growth (NSFG). The major controls used in these tables are race and age and no tests of statistical significance are presented. These data are included to provide a description of the characteristics of adolescent parents. Caution should be used in drawing conclusions from these tables on consequences of adolescent parenthood.

TABLE 8.1 Percent of Women Aged 20-29 Completing High School By Age At Birth Of First Child, Race And Ethnicity*, 1982 National Survey of Family Growth

	Age at First Birth	Percent of Women 20-29 Completing Less Than 12 Years of Schooling	
		Percent	Number of Women
Total Mothers		25	(1739)
	Under 15	68	(42)
	15-17	51	(424)
	18-19	34	(467)
	20-21	19	(358)
	22-24	10	(312)
	25-29	5	(133)
Women with no births		7	(1252)
White	Total Mothers	26	(764)
	Under 15	--	(2)
	15-17	55	(116)
	18-19	39	(170)
	20-21	21	(181)
	22-24	10	(204)
	25-29	5	(90)
Women with no births		6	(820)
Black	Total Mothers	26	(942)
	Under 15	62	(40)
	15-17	43	(304)
	18-19	23	(286)
	20-21	11	(172)
	22-24	8	(101)
	25-29	0	(37)
Women with no births		9	(404)
Hispanic	Total Mothers	58	(113)
	Under 15	--	(0)
	15-17	76	(23)
	18-19	69	(21)
	20-21	55	(38)
	22-24	39	(24)
	25-29	--	(7)
Women with no births		17	(51)

-- Cell sizes were less than 20.

*Hispanic Persons may be of any race, and whites and blacks may include Hispanic persons.

Source: Special tabulations from the 1982 National Survey of Family Growth, Cycle III, conducted by the National Center for Health Statistics, DHHS.

TABLE 8.1

Table 8.1 shows the percent of women aged 20 to 29 completing less than 12 years of schooling by age at first birth, race and ethnicity. The data are from the 1982 National Survey of Family Growth (NSFG).

In general, women who had a first birth before age 20 were considerably more likely to complete less than 12 years of schooling than women who gave birth at age 20 or later. The percent of women completing less than 12 years of schooling was 68 percent for those under aged 15, 51 percent for those aged 15 to 17, and 34 percent for women aged 18 to 19 at first birth, compared to 19 percent of women aged 20 to 21, 10 percent of women aged 22 to 24 and 5 percent of women aged 25 to 29 at first birth.

Additionally, white and Hispanic women with age at first birth less than 20 were more likely to complete less than 12 years of schooling than black women. For instance, 55 percent of the white women and 76 percent of the Hispanic women aged 15 to 17 at first birth completed less than 12 years of schooling compared to 43 percent of the black women aged 15 to 17 at first birth.

TABLE 8.2 Percent of Mothers Aged 20-29 Having A Subsequent Birth Within 24 Months Of The First, By Their Age at First Birth, Race And Ethnicity*, 1982 National Survey of Family Growth

	Age at First Birth	% of Women 20-24 w/2nd Birth Within 24 Months of 1st (n)		% of Women 25-29 w/2nd Birth Within 24 Months of 1st (N)		% of Women 20-29 w/2nd Birth Within 24 Months of 1st (N)	
		Percent	Number of Women	Percent	Number of Women	Percent	Number of Women
Total	All Mothers	17	(653)	18	(1086)	18	(1739)
	Under 15	18	(24)	--	(18)	16	(42)
	15-17	18	(187)	20	(237)	19	(424)
	18-19	25	(203)	24	(264)	25	(467)
	20-21	14	(167)	17	(191)	15	(358)
	22-24	7	(71)	18	(241)	16	(312)
	25-29	n.a.	n.a.	11	(133)	11	(133)
White	Total	18	(262)	17	(502)	18	(764)
	Under 15	--	(2)	--	(0)	--	(2)
	15-17	16	(51)	17	(65)	16	(116)
	18-19	27	(78)	24	(92)	26	(170)
	20-21	15	(87)	18	(94)	16	(181)
	22-24	8	(44)	18	(160)	15	(204)
	25-29	n.a.	n.a.	10	(90)	10	(90)
Black	Total	17	(380)	21	(562)	19	(942)
	Under 15	20	(22)	--	(18)	16	(40)
	15-17	25	(134)	28	(170)	27	(304)
	18-19	17	(120)	24	(166)	20	(286)
	20-21	9	(77)	13	(95)	11	(172)
	22-24	4	(26)	19	(75)	15	(101)
	25-29	n.a.	n.a.	10	(37)	10	(37)
Hispanic	Total	11	(34)	20	(79)	16	(113)
	Under 15	--	(0)	--	(0)	--	(0)
	15-17	--	(9)	--	(14)	14	(23)
	18-19	--	(6)	--	(15)	34	(21)
	20-21	--	(15)	9	(23)	13	(38)
	22-24	--	(4)	14	(20)	11	(24)
	25-29	n.a.	n.a.	--	(7)	--	(7)

--Cell sizes were les than 20.

*Hispanic persons may be of any race, and whites and blacks may include Hispanic persons.

n.a. - not applicable.

Source: Special tabulations from the 1982 National Survey of Family Growth, conducted by the National Center for Health Statistics, DHHS.

TABLE 8.2

Table 8.2 shows the percent of women aged 20 to 29 having a subsequent birth within 24 months by their age at first birth. The data are from the 1982 National Survey of Family Growth (NSFG).

Among women aged 20 to 29, 19 percent of the blacks, 18 percent of the whites and 16 percent of the Hispanics had a second birth within 24 months of the first. The highest percent having a second birth among white and Hispanic women aged 20 to 29 were women who first gave birth at age 18 or 19, 25 and 34 percent respectively. Among black women however, women who first gave birth at ages 15 to 17 were the most likely to have a second birth within 24 months.

In general, women who first gave birth before age 20 were at least as likely, and in some cases more likely, than women aged 20 to 29 at first birth to have a second birth within 24 months of the first.

TABLE 8.3 Cumulative Percentage Of Metropolitan-Area Women Aged 15-19 Who Had A Premarital Second Pregnancy, By Number Of Months Following Outcome Of The Premarital First Pregnancy, According To Race, Outcome And Age At Conclusion Of First Pregnancy, 1971, 1976 And 1979

Months After 1st Outcome by Year	Total	Race		Outcome		Age	
		White	Black	Birth	Abortion	≤16	17-19
1971	(N=214)	(N=36)	(N=178)	(N=173)	(N=41)	(N=110)	(N=104)
6	7.8	0.0	12.4	8.2	6.6	7.8	7.9
12	12.4	2.2	18.0	13.2	9.6	14.4	9.4
18	23.0	10.5	29.0	23.1	23.3	21.5	30.1
24	33.1	31.7	33.9	23.8	60.6	33.3	30.1
1976	(N=175)	(N=50)	(N=125)	(N=126)	(N=49)	(N=100)	(N=75)
6	7.5	8.4	6.3	6.7	8.4	4.2	10.7
12	19.9	17.1	21.9	23.4	13.0	20.7	17.5
18	27.2	17.1	34.4	33.4	15.0	26.2	28.5
24	36.0	26.2	42.8	36.0	39.3	31.7	44.4
1979	(N=290)	(N=110)	(N=180)	(N=169)	(N=121)	(N=181)	(N=109)
6	6.4	6.3	6.6	3.7	9.0	6.0	6.6
12	17.5	18.2	16.1	17.1	18.0	15.2	22.9
18	23.8	24.7	22.3	25.5	22.8	21.2	30.7
24	30.7	29.8	32.7	37.8	25.1	29.3	30.7

Source: M.A. Koenig and M. Zelnik. "Repeat Pregnancies Among Metropolitan Area Teenagers: 1971-1979," Family Planning Perspectives 14 (6) (November/December), Table 2, 1982. Reprinted by permission.

TABLE 8.3

Table 8.3 presents the cumulative percentage of metropolitan-area women aged 15 to 19 who reported a second premarital pregnancy, by the number of months following the outcome of the first premarital pregnancy, by race, outcome, and age at conclusion of first pregnancy. Data are from the 1971, 1976 and 1979 National Surveys of Young Women (NSFG) in which we recognize abortions are under-reported.

A higher cumulative percent of black teens reported a second premarital pregnancy within 24 months after the outcome of the first premarital pregnancy than white teens in 1971, 1976 and 1979. Among white teens 32 percent in 1971, 26 percent in 1976 and 30 percent in 1979 reported second pregnancies within 24 months while among the black teens 34 percent in 1971, 43 percent in 1976 and 33 percent in 1979 had second pregnancies within 24 months.

Among black teens, 34 percent in 1971, 43 percent in 1976 and 33 percent in 1979 had a second premarital pregnancies within two years of the outcome of the first premarital pregnancy.

Among women who reported a first premarital birth the cumulative percent having a second pregnancy within 24 months was 24 percent in 1971, 36 percent in 1976 and 38 percent in 1979. The cumulative percent of those reporting a first premarital abortion who became pregnant a second time within 24 months after the abortion was 25 percent in 1979, 39 percent in 1976 and 61 percent in 1971.

By 24 months after the resolution of a first premarital pregnancy, more women under age 16 than women aged 17 to 19 had a second pregnancy in 1971, 33 compared to 30 percent.

In contrast, in 1976 and 1979 more women aged 17 to 19 than age 16 or under had a second pregnancy: 44 and 32 percent in 1976, and 31 and 29 percent in 1979.

TABLE 8.4 Receipt Of AFDC Among Women Aged 20-29 By The Women's Age At First Birth, Race, And Ethnicity*, 1982 National Survey Of Family Growth

	Age at First Birth	Percent of Women 20-29 Receiving Any AFDC Income	
		Percent	Number of Women
Total	All Mothers	13	(1739)
	Under 15	45	(42)
	15-17	20	(424)
	18-19	21	(467)
	20-21	14	(358)
	22-24	3	(312)
	25-29	2	(133)
	Women with no births	1	(1252)
White	All Mothers	9	(764)
	Under 15	--	(2)
	15-17	12	(116)
	18-19	17	(170)
	20-21	10	(181)
	22-24	2	(204)
	25-29	1	(90)
	Women with no births	1	(820)
Black	All Mothers	33	(942)
	Under 15	53	(40)
	15-17	39	(304)
	18-19	31	(286)
	20-21	36	(172)
	22-24	15	(101)
	25-29	9	(37)
	Women with no births	4	(404)
Hispanic	All Mothers	12	(113)
	Under 15	--	(0)
	15-17	9	(23)
	18-19	25	(21)
	20-21	18	(38)
	22-24	1	(24)
	25-29	--	(7)
	Women with no births	3	(51)

--Cell sizes were less than 20.

*Hispanic persons may be of any race and whites and blacks may include Hispanic persons.

n.a. - not applicable.

Source: Special tabulations from the 1982 National Survey of Family Growth, Cycle III, conducted by the National Center for Health Statistics, DHHS.

TABLE 8.4

Table 8.4 shows the percentage distribution of mothers aged 20 to 29 receiving Aid for Dependent Children (AFDC) by age at first birth, race and ethnicity. Data are from the 1982 National Survey of Family Growth (NSFG).

Overall, 13 percent of all mothers aged 20 to 29 received AFDC; 9 percent of the white mothers, 12 percent of hispanic mothers and 33 percent of black mothers. Mothers who were under age 20 at first birth were more likely to be receiving AFDC than those over age 20 at first birth. Forty-five percent of the mothers who were under age 15, 20 percent who were aged 15 to 17, and 21 percent who were aged 18 to 19 at the birth of their first child, compared to 14 percent who were aged 20 to 21, 3 percent who were age 22 to 24 and 2 percent who were age 25 to 29 at the birth of their first child were receiving AFDC in 1982.

TABLE 8.5 Poverty* Status Of Women Aged 20-29, By Their Age At First Birth, Race, and Ethnicity**, 1982 National Survey of Family Growth

	Age at First Birth	Percent of Women 20-29 Receiving Any AFDC Income	
		Percent	Number of Women
Total	Total Mothers	36	(1739)
	Under 15	78	(42)
	15-17	50	(424)
	18-19	51	(467)
	20-21	37	(358)
	22-24	20	(312)
	25-29	9	(133)
Women with no births		23	(1252)
White	Total Mothers	32	(764)
	Under 15	--	(2)
	15-17	45	(116)
	18-19	47	(170)
	20-21	34	(181)
	22-24	19	(204)
	25-29	7	(90)
Women with no births		21	(820)
Black	Total Mothers	57	(942)
	Under 15	76	(40)
	15-17	63	(304)
	18-19	62	(286)
	20-21	56	(172)
	22-24	30	(101)
	25-29	16	(37)
Women with no births		34	(404)
Hispanic	Total Mothers	48	(113)
	Under 15	--	(0)
	15-17	60	(23)
	18-19	58	(21)
	20-21	42	(38)
	22-24	42	(24)
	25-29	--	(7)
Women with no births		27	(51)

--Cell sizes were less than 20.

*The definition of poverty is the woman's family income divided by the Census Bureau's poverty threshold, specific for family size.
**Hispanic Persons may be of any race and whites and blacks may include Hispanic Persons.

n.a. - not applicable.

Source: Special tabulations from the 1982 National Survey of Family Growth, Cycle III, conducted by the National Center for Health Statistics, DHHS.

TABLE 8.5

Table 8.5 shows the percent of mothers aged 20 to 29 whose incomes were 150 percent less than the poverty level by age at birth of first child, race and ethnicity. These data are from the 1982 National Survey of Family Growth.

Of all mothers aged 20 to 29, 36 percent had incomes below 150 percent of the poverty level; 32 percent of the white mothers, 48 percent of the Hispanic mothers and 57 percent of the black mothers. Of the women under age 15, aged 15 to 17 and aged 18 to 19 at first birth, 78, 50 and 51 percent respectively had incomes below 150 percent of the poverty level compared to 37, 20 and 9 percent of women aged 20 to 21, 22 to 24 and 25 to 29 at first birth.

Additionally, 23 percent of the women who had no births had incomes below 150 percent of the poverty level; 34 percent of black women, 27 percent of the hispanic women and 21 percent of the white women.

ADDENDUM

COMMONLY USED DATA SOURCES

This addendum contains descriptions of commonly used sources. These are listed below along with their acronyms.

NSFG	1.	National Survey of Family Growth
NLS	2.	National Longitudinal Surveys of Labor Market Experience of Youth; Young Women, Young Men, Mature Women and Mature Men
	3.	National Vital Statistics
CPS	4.	Current Population Surveys; and Fertility Supplements
	5.	National Survey of Young Women (and Young Men); Kantner-Zelnick Data.
AGI	6.	Alan Guttmacher Institute
NCHS	7.	National Center for Health Statistics--collects the vital statistics on births
CDC	8.	Center for Disease Control

A-154 / 506

TITLE The National Survey of Family Growth (NSFG)

PURPOSE The National Survey of Family Growth is a primary source of data on U.S. fertility patterns, infertility, reproductive health, contraception, and fertility intentions. In addition, the Survey obtains information relevant to child development on such topics as unwanted childbearing, adoption, adolescent pregnancy and unwed motherhood, prenatal care, post-natal care, and infant health. These topics may be examined in relation to information obtained on a variety of social, economic, and family characteristics. In addition, because the NSFG represents the continuation of a line of fertility surveys extending back to 1955, it is possible to use the data to continue a set of time-series statistics on family building, contraceptive use, and reproductive health that has covered a period of dramatic change in U.S. family patterns. Data from these surveys have also been used for several studies of changes in family composition. Data are used by health care providers and researchers, demographers and other social scientists, and by policy makers at both the federal and local level.

SPONSORSHIP The survey is sponsored by the National Center for Health Statistics, Division of Vital Statistics, Family Growth Survey Branch. Funding has been provided by the Office of Family Planning Services in the (then) Bureau of Community Health Services, the Center for Population Research, NICHD, the Office of Adolescent Programs, as well as NCHS.

DESIGN Women aged 15 to 44 of all marital statuses are interviewed in the nationally representative NSFG. The area probability sample of approximately 8,000 women in 1982 included an over-sample of 1,900 teenagers. Parental consent is obtained for all minors who are interviewed. Separate questionnaires are designed for women under age 25 and 25 and older. The 1982 interview--Cycle III of the NSFG--was the first to include all women in the childbearing years regardless of their marital status. Blacks were over-sampled to enable separate analyses of blacks.

A change in fieldwork is planned for the 1986 survey. To reduce costs, the sample will be selected on the basis of screening questions included in the large and nationally representative Health Interview Survey.

PERIODICITY
The NSFG provides data that continue a statistical time-series on American fertility patterns that was initiated during the early years of the "baby boom". The Growth of American Families surveys took place in 1955 and 1960 and were continued by the National Fertility Studies of 1965 and 1970. Cycles I, II, and III of the NSFG were fielded in 1973, 1976, and 1982 respectively. Cycle IV is scheduled for 1987.

CONTENT
Detailed data are collected on fertility events, on infertility and contraceptive use, on childbearing plans, adoption, and sex education, on reproductive and infant health, pre-natal and post-natal care, and family composition. Considerable background information is also collected on the women and their families.

LIMITATIONS
Since the focus of the Survey is on fertility the range of information on females under 15 and males 15-19 is limited. Under-reporting of abortion occurs in this, as in other household surveys. Since this is a survey of women, children living only with fathers are not represented.

Surveys prior to 1982 do not include teens who were not married or their mothers. This restricts trend analyses that can be done.

AVAILABILITY
Public use data tapes are available for the entire series of national surveys from the National Technical Information Service.

Contact: Dr. William Pratt,
Chief, Survey of Family Growth Branch
National Center for Health Statistics
3700 East-West Highway
Hyattsville, MD 20782
301-436-8731

A-156 / 508

TITLE National Longitudinal Survey of the Labor Market Experience of Youth

PURPOSE In 1977, it was decided to both continue the existing panels of the National Longitudinal Survey and to expand data collection by initiating a new National Longitudinal Survey of Youth. Data from the new survey would replicate much of the information obtained on young people in the earlier cohorts and would thus support studies of changes in the labor market experience of youth. In addition, the new data on youth would permit evaluation of the expanded employment and training programs for youth established by the 1977 amendments to the Comprehensive Employment and Training Act (CETA). The supplementary sample of 1,300 persons serving in the Armed Forces permit a study of the recruitment and service experiences of youth in the military. The richness of the data has also attracted researchers studying fertility issues, educational progress, marriage and divorce, income family structure.

SPONSORSHIP The Department of Labor initiated the National Longitudinal Surveys and has provided much of the funding over the years. However, other agencies including the National Institute of Child Health and Human Development, the National Institute on Drug Abuse, the National Institute on Alcohol and Alcohol Abuse, and the Department of Defense have sponsored portions of the survey. Data are collected by the National Opinion Research Center.

DESIGN The Youth sample is comprised of a nationally-representative probability sample of 5,700 young women and an equal number of young men 14-21, as of January 1, 1979, augmented by a sample of 1,300 young persons serving in the Armed Forces. Blacks, hispanics, and disadvantaged whites were all over-sampled to facilitate analysis of youth in these population groups. Individuals were considered to be in the population if they resided within the 50 states and were not institutionalized, or if they were on active military duty outside the United States. Non-military respondents were selected using a multistage, stratified area probability sample of dwelling units and group quarter units. A screening interview was administered at approximately 75,000 dwellings and group quarters in 202 primary sampling unites. Military respondents were sampled from rosters provided by the Department of Defense. A total of 12,686 persons were interviewed. As of the completion of the fifth (1984) interview wave, 96 percent of those interviewed in 1979 were still being interviewed.

PERIODICITY   Interviews have been conducted annually since 1979. Interviews are currently planned to continue at least through 1985.

CONTENT   The National Longitudinal Surveys were designed primarily to analyze sources of variation in the labor market behavior and experience of Americans. Consequently, the content of the surveys is weighted toward labor force training and experience. However a great deal of information is also collected regarding formal education, marriage and fertility events, income and assets, family background, attitudes, aspirations, and expectations. Questions on drug and alcohol use are included, as well, along with information on family planning, child care, and maternal and child health care.

LIMITATIONS   There is under reporting of abortion, pregnancies and births.

AVAILABILITY   Public use tapes and tape documentation as well as a list of publications are available from the Center for Human Resource Research, 5701 North High Street, Worthington, Ohio 43085.

Contact: Frank Mott with questions regarding data on fertility and maternal and child health (612) 422-7337. Information is also available from Pat Rhoton or Dennis Grey or Ken Wolpin, Principal Investigator for the NLS, (614) 422-7337

A-158 / 510

TITLE — National Longitudinal Surveys of the Labor Market Experience of: Young Women, Young Men, Mature Women, and Mature Men

PURPOSE — This series of longitudinal surveys was initiated to explore the labor market experiences over time of several unique cohorts facing employment problems of particular concern to policy makers. The school-to-work transition, initial occupational choice, adaptation to the work of work, the work-family interface and attainment of stable employment are issues of concern for the cohorts of young men, aged 14-24 in 1966 and young women, aged 14-24 in 1968. For middle aged men, aged 45-59 in 1966, issues of declining health, unemployment, the obsolescence of skills, and age discrimination are of concern. Among women 30-44 in 1967, the key issue initially was labor force re-entry for women as their children became older. Subsequently, issues associated with women's retirement became important. Following these cohorts over time enables analysts both to describe the situations of different population groups and to understand the factors that are antecedents and consequences of situations ranging from education and employment, to marriage and family, to economic status.

SPONSORSHIP — These four longitudinal surveys were initiated by the Office of Manpower Policy Evaluation, and Research of the Department of Labor. The Center for Human Research of Ohio State University has developed the questionnaires and makes computer tapes and a wide range of documentation available. Field work is conducted by the U.S. Bureau of the Census.

DESIGN — Each of the four age-sex cohorts is represented by a multi-stage probability sample. To provide samples of blacks that would produce statistically reliable statistics, households in enumeration districts that were primarily black were sampled at a rate between three and four times that of other households. From over 35,000 inhabited housing units, a sample of 5050 men 45-59 was interviewed. A sample of 5225 males 14-24, excluding males on active military service was interviewed. Five thousand eight-three women, 30-44, and 5,159 young women 14-24 were also interviewed. The total number of households represented in the four NLS samples is 13,582; thus the sample includes a number of families that have contributed more than one respondent. Initially, most interviews were conducted in person; however the majority of the interviews conducted in person; however the majority of the interviews conducted during the 1970s were done on the telephone. Data have been weighted to adjust for over-sam- pling and for sample attrition; when weighted, the data are nationally representative. As of the 15-year interview points, approximately 56 percent of the males originally 45-59, 65 percent of the younger men, and about 70 percent of the two women's cohorts interviewed initially were still being interviewed.

PERIODICITY   Young women were interviewed annually between 1968 and 1973, in 1975, 1977, 1978, 1980, 1982, 1983 and 1985. Further interviews are planned for 1987 and 1988.

Women were interviewed annually between 1967-69, in 1971-1972, 1974, 1976, 1977, 1979, 1981, 1982, and 1984. Interviews are tentatively planned for 1986 and 1987.

Young men were interviewed annually between 1966 and 1971, in 1975, 1976, 1978, 1980, and 1983. Further interviews have been cancelled.

Men were interviewed annually between 1966 and 1969, in 1971, 1973, 1975, 1976, 1978, 1980, 1981, and 1983. Further interviews have been cancelled.

CONTENT   In keeping with the primary orientation of the surveys toward labor force issues, numerous questions focus on employment experience, unemployment, income, and training. However, quite a bit of information was collected about the family background and the social and economic status of the family as well. None of the respondents were still children after the mid-1970s; however, a majority of the young women and young men had become parents by the 1980s, and some limited information is available about their children. Considerable information, shown below, was collected on the family situation of the young men and young women respondents when they were growing up.

AVAILABILITY   Data tapes and complete documentation as well as a
              publications list are available from the Center for
              Human Resource Research, 5701 North High Street,
              Worthington, Ohio 43085.

              Contact: Pat Rhoton or the respective cohort
                        coordinators:
                        Mature men - Gilbert Nestel
                        Mature women - Lois Shaw
                        Young men - Stephen Hills
                        Young women - Frank Mott, or Principal
                        Investigator for the NLS - Ken Wolpin (514)
                        888-8238 or (614) 422-7337

TITLE	Vital Statistics of the United States--Natality
PURPOSE	The purpose of the natality reporting system is to collect and tabulate at the federal level data on births from the 50 states and the District of Columbia. Demographic and health information can be analyzed by researchers and policymakers interested in assessing the health of infants and pinpointing health problems, making population projections and estimates, and measuring progress made by national health programs. In addition, the birth certificate provides legal proof of the birth.
SPONSORSHIP	The National Center for Health Statistics, vital Statistics Division, collects and publishes natality data.
DESIGN	Data are collected at the local level and forwarded to the state level. States report the data to the Division of Vital Statistics. A certificate for all live births and for stillbirths is completed by the attending physician or other health personnel. One hundred percent of the births are reported to NCHS in 42 states and 50 percent are reported in the remaining areas.
PERIODICITY	Data collection is continuous. Monthly and annual reports are issued.
CONTENT	The certificate of live birth, which is the source of vital registration data, contains a limited number of items. The mother's marital status is reported for only 41 states and D.C.; as of 1980 it is inferred for 9 states by comparing parent and child surnames. Parent educations is reported for 47 states and D.C.
LIMITATIONS	Not all states obtain all information and the range of data is limited (see above).

AVAILABILITY   Data tapes may be purchased from the National Technical Information Service (703) 487-4780.

Contact: Stephanie Ventura, Selma Taffel or Bob Heuser, Chief (301) 436-8954, Natality Branch, Division of Vital Statistics, National Center for Health Statistics, 3700 East-West Highway, Hyattsville, Maryland 20792

TITLE   Current Population Survey

PURPOSE   The primary purpose of The Current Population Survey is
                  to provide monthly measures of the characteristics of
                  the labor force, labor force participation, employment,
                  and unemployment in the United States as well as indi-
                  vidual states and regions. In addition the survey ser-
                  ves as a vehicle for a series of supplements, conducted
                  with varying degrees of regularity. Recent supplements
                  have included job tenure and occupational mobility
                  (January), demographic and income supplement (March),
                  alimony and child support (April), multiple job holding
                  (May), fertility (June), immunization (September),
                  school enrollment (October), and voting and registra-
                  tion (November). These supplements are not necessarily
                  conducted each year. For example, the voting and regis-
                  tration supplements are conducted only in elections
                  years.

SPONSORSHIP   The core survey is funded by the U.S. Department of
                  Labor, which is responsible for its content. The
                  Supplements are funded by a variety of sponsors, such
                  as the National Institute of Child Health and Human
                  Development (some of the fertility and childcare sup-
                  plements) and the National Center for Education Sta-
                  tistics (the education supplements). The data are
                  collected by the U.S. Bureau of the Census.

DESIGN   The survey is designed to be representative of all per-
                  sons age 14 or over living in households in the United
                  States. More specifically it covers the civilian non-
                  institutional population plus armed forces personnel
                  living off-base or living on base with their families.
                  A multi-stage probability sampling method is used in-
                  volving first the selection of geographically defined
                  primary sampling units (629 in 1982), next (through
                  sub-stages) the selection of households within sampling
                  units (63,000 households in 1982), and finally the iden-
                  tification of all persons 14 and over in sample house-
                  holds. In 1983, interviews, conducted in person, were
                  obtained in 60,000 of the 63,000 households selected.
                  The sample is designed to cover each of the 50 states
                  and the District of Columbia.

                  The sample is slowly changed through the use of rotation
                  groups. Any given rotation group is in the sample for

4 months, leaves the sample for 8 months, and returns for a final 4 months. In any given month the sample is composed of households from 8 different rotation groups.

PERIODICITY The survey was begun in 1940 and has been conducted monthly since then. For the purpose of measuring employment, that week which contains the 12th of the month is used as a reference week.

CONTENT In addition to data on employment, unemployment, personal income, and work-related activities, the core survey collects data on family income, housing tenure, household composition, age, sex, education, race/origin, and marital status.

AVAILABILITY A rich array of published tabulations are available in The Current Population Reports, especially Series P-20 (population characteristics), Series P-23 (special studies), Series P-25 (population estimates and projections) and P-60 (consumer income).

Machine-readable micro data files are available from the Bureau of the Census for most months (for information about the availability of data for a particular month, inquiry may be made at Customer Services). Each file contains the data for a particular month. The first year for which files are available is 1968. Files for March are typically available 3-4 months after the survey date. The delay for other months may be longer.

Contact: Greg Weiland 301/763-2773
Data Users Services Division: Customer Services 301/763-4100

TITLE	Current Population Survey-Fertility Supplements
PURPOSE	The fertility supplements are designed to provide national estimates of women's fertility and expectations for future births. In addition some supplements (1977, 1982) have provided information about the child care arrangements used by working mothers for their youngest child under age 5.
SPONSORSHIP	The fertility and birth expectations portions of the supplement are entirely a project of the U.S. Bureau of the Census. The child care portions of the 1977 supplement was sponsored by the Department of Health and Human Services and an expanded fertility supplement in 1980 was jointly sponsored by the Bureau and the National Institute of Child Health and Human Development.
DESIGN	A description of the basic design of the Current Population Survey was provided in the write-up of the core survey. The supplemental questions have been asked of all persons in sampled households meeting certain eligibility requirements. Most recently these criteria are being an never-married female age 15-59 or a never married female age 18-59. Birth expectation questions are asked of women 18-44. However, these age criteria have varied from as low as age 14 to as high as age 75. In the expanded fertility supplement marital history data were gathered on men age 15-75 as well as women.
PERIODICITY	The supplement has been conducted each June since 1971. A supplement is planned for 1984.
CONTENT	Each supplement collects data on fertility and birth expectations. In addition the 1971, 1975, and 1980 supplements provide data on marriages and child spacing; and the 1977 and 1982 supplements, on child care. The 1980 supplement for the first time collected data on the marriage histories of men as well as of women, and included questions about men's children under 18 from previous marriages and whether any of these children live elsewhere.

LIMITATIONS   The usual supplement is quite brief, only providing
data on total number of births, the birthdate of the
youngest (sometimes also the oldest) child, and the
number of additional children expected. The child care
sections in 1977 and 1982 cover only child care arrangements of working mothers with children under 5, and for
only the youngest of these children. Data are gathered
on the kind of payment (cash or non-cash) but not the
amount. The exclusion of unmarried women under 18 from
any of the supplements means that no data on out-of-
wedlock births to younger teenagers are available from
this source.

Analyses of data from the marriage histories have shown
that such retrospective histories are subject to considerable error, especially with regard to events
several years in the past. The survey's practice of
obtaining information from proxy respondents undoubtedly
compounds this effect. Since most respondents are
women, the data for men are most seriously affected.

Comparisons with other sources of data also show that
the reports of men's children from previous marriages
living elsewhere are too low.

AVAILABILITY   Refer to the description of the core survey. Machine-
readable micro-data files are available for June from
1973. The latest tape currently available containing
data from the June supplement is for 1982.

TITLE	The National Surveys of Young Women and Men (Kantner-Zelnik data)
PURPOSE	The Kantner-Zelnik studies have been a primary source of data on sexual experience of U.S. females between the ages of 15 and 19 during the 1970's and males age 17 to 21 in 1979. In addition, the three surveys (1971, 1976, and 1979) collected information on contraceptive use, pregnancies, pregnancy intention, and sex education experience.
SPONSORSHIP	John I. Kantner and Melvin Zelnik have been the principal investigators of these surveys. Funding has been provided by the Center for Population Research, NICHD, the Ford Foundation, and General Services Foundation.
DESIGN	The designs have differed slightly for the three interviews. The 1971 survey interviewed 15-19 year old women living in households in the continental United States, N=4611, and by means of a separate sample, young women living in college dormitories, total N=4611, and by means of a separate sample, young women living in college dormitories, total N=219. The 1976 survey sampled 2500 women born between March 1956 and February 1961 (age 15-19) living in households in the continental United States. The 1979 survey included both young women and young men living in households in Standard Metropolitan Statistical Areas (SMSAs) in the continental United States. Eligible female respondents were born between March 1959 and February 1964 (ages 15-19), total N=1,717, and eligible men between March 1957 and February 1962, total N=917.
PERIODICITY	Interviews have been conducted in three different years: 1971, 1976 and 1979. There have been different respondents in each cohort.
CONTENT	Detailed data are collected on sexual activity, contraceptive use, pregnancy, pregnancy intention, and sex education experience. Some background information was also collected.
LIMITATIONS	Under-reporting of abortions, pregnancies and births.

TITLE	Alan Guttmacher Institute (AGI)
PURPOSE	The Alan Guttmacher Institute is a primary source of data on U.S. abortion services. The AGI has surveyed all identified abortion providers in each state each year since 1973.
SPONSORSHIP	The Alan Guttmacher Institute, which receives support from a variety of private foundations.
DESIGN	All identified abortion providers in each state are surveyed.
PERIODICITY	The survey has covered each year from 1973-1982.
CONTENT	Data on age, race, marital status, education, number of children, gestation at abortion, number of previous abortions, and method of abortion are obtained from the Centers for Disease Control and combined with AGI data on the total number of abortions to generate national estimates.